The Scottish Football Book No 22

Hot action in the Scottish Cup Final as
Hearts' Jim Brown tries to stop Rangers'
Derek Johnstone, the man with the killer
shot.

THE SCOTTISH FOOTBALL BOOK NO 22

Edited by Hugh Taylor

Stanley Paul, London

Stanley Paul & Co Ltd
3 Fitzroy Square London W1

An imprint of the Hutchinson Publishing Group

London Melbourne Sydney Auckland
Wellington Johannesburg and agencies
throughout the world

First published 1976
© Stanley Paul & Co Ltd 1976

Printed in Great Britain by litho by
The Anchor Press Ltd and bound by
Wm Brendon & Son Ltd both of
Tiptree, Essex

ISBN 0 09 127460 5

CONTENTS

THE EDITOR SAYS...

The European Cup Final between Bayern Munich of West Germany and St Etienne of France at Hampden Park on 12 May 1976, brought colour, excitment and a Continental atmosphere to dear grey old Glasgow.

It also brought the biggest argument of an intriguing season: Should Scotland try to alter her football technique, attempt to play in the Bayern way?

Certainly Bayern flew home with the European Cup; certainly, by winning the trophy for the third successive year they proved themselves to be the best side in Europe, if not in the world.

But they were not exciting.

They have rare skill, of course. But they play within themselves. They don't extend themselves to the limits in a bid to win gloriously – and that kind of technical football the British just don't like.

The Scots at Hampden felt that St Etienne, who lost 1–0, were the heroes. They tried so valiantly, they had most of the attack, but they missed chances. Then Bayern scored – and went back into their shell. They were cynical. Said their coach, Dettmar Kramer: 'It is a cup final so one must win it – one cannot afford to lose.'

That attitude disappointed the Scots who felt Bayern, magnificent in terms of skill, could have played much better if they had wanted to. Yet Bayern won. And isn't football about winning?

Frankly, I don't think so. Sure, you want your team to get a good victory. But you also want to see dramatic, exciting, flowing football. And although modern British coaches argue that our football should now be played in the Continental way, with patience the main virtue and players refusing to go all-out, I feel our more vigorous soccer is still what our fans want to see – win or lose.

The trouble with teams like Bayern is that they snuff out the candle of other sides' flair and ambition and make technical skill the be-all and end-all of football which should really be a brawny, brainy game of effort. Continental fans, used to the patient approach, are content to accept this unauthorized version of our great game but I consider this approach strips the cloak of glamour from football and clads it in denims.

Of course, we could try to copy the splendid passing and ball control of Bayern but I hope that our teams never become as cynical as the Germans, that we continue to be entertained by wonderful wingers, dashing leaders, inspired inside-forwards and players who will attack until they die.

Perhaps our new-look Scotland international team have the right method. Gone are the bristling bantams, the death-or-glory outlook the men in blue used to consider was the only style for a Scotland team.

Manager Willie Ormond has evolved a new pattern which contains much of the best of the Continental style and the golden threads of old Scottish football. It's attrac-

7

tive and entertaining and shows that clever, up-to-date football doesn't have to be ruthless, cynical or dull.

Although Rangers covered themselves in glory by winning all the Scottish major honours, it was an exciting season and the new Premier League made a promising start.

Can the League be improved? There were moves to allow 12 clubs to take part in the major League but I consider it shouldn't be altered until it has a chance to prove itself – or otherwise.

The big question for the season is: Can anyone topple Rangers? It won't be easy for Rangers are playing with assurance. But now that manager Jock Stein, recovered from his car accident, is back at Parkhead there will be an even tougher challenge from Celtic, and Motherwell, who came so close to being a great side last season, should be even better with that fierce season behind them.

As always, Scotland produced a splendid crop of players again. While mighty John Greig was chosen as Scotland's Player of the Year, he was run close by Celtic's Danny McGrain, that outstanding back who simply can't play a bad game.

And new names crept into the headlines – winger Malcolm Robertson, of Ayr United, Martin Henderson, of Rangers, Roy Aitken, of Celtic, among them. Keep an eye on these lads. They're going to be really good.

As always, too, a warm welcome to the new Scottish Football Book. I hope you enjoy it.

Hugh Taylor

BLUE HEAVEN
Rangers win the Treble

Only 22 seconds had gone. But a Dundee United defender slipped. That was enough for Derek Johnstone, the deadliest striker in football. He swept in, got to the ball first – and slammed it into the United net.

What a goal that was – for it was the goal which gave Rangers the first Premier League championship. And season 1975–6 went down in football history as one of the greatest Rangers had ever known. The men of Ibrox had at last stepped out of the huge black shadow which had dogged them over the last decade.

The lightning goal in conjunction with Celtic's home defeat by Ayr United gave Rangers the title they richly deserved. In the end, they were out on their own. For a time, the Premier League looked highly competitive. Gradually, however, Motherwell and Hibernian faltered. That left the new division a two-horse race between Rangers and Celtic. But Rangers kept going on strongly. And Celtic stumbled near the finish.

Rangers pinned their faith on attack – and they were rewarded. Manager Jock Wallace admitted later that he took a gamble. 'We were going through a bad spell,' he said, 'and I decided the only thing to do was to play an attacking game and to hell with worrying about keeping opponents out.'

This policy came into effect after Rangers had been humiliated by St Etienne in the European Cup.

And that policy showed what a big club Rangers are. Only a club as proud and determined as Rangers could have picked themselves up off the floor as they did in the bad days of autumn, roll up their sleeves and find a knock-out punch. Rangers won the League Cup – and never looked back.

They found a settled side. Former Hibernian player Johnny Hamilton was brought into the team as the midfield purveyor. Four forwards were thrown permanently into the attack. And Rangers concentrated more on artistry than power. Character – Jock Wallace's favourite word – began to emerge.

'I know it took us a long time to get our nose in front,' said the Ibrox manager, 'but I never doubted that we would.' Then Jock added his own philosophy: 'Where I come from in Wallyford they're miners and there's a saying, "Have no fear of straight men". In their terms it means never leave a loose prop in case it falls on the next man. That's how we work at Ibrox – straight.'

The entire Rangers staff, first team, reserves, youngsters, management, meet every week and in these seminars all problems are public. Money is never mentioned. And Rangers won the title because of the players' dedication – and the enthusiasm of their manager.

Wallace can't do enough for his players. He says: 'My own satisfaction is not in seeing them win every Saturday but seeing them get on. There's no greater honour in this game than playing for Scotland – and that happened during this great season for Alex MacDonald, Bobby McKean, Tom Forsyth, who might not have expected it at the start of the term, and for John Greig, too, although he's a veteran.'

How the Rangers players responded to

9

Jock Wallace, the manager who inspired Rangers.

How good were Rangers? The best in Scotland undoubtedly. But they were shown up by St Etienne, although they would have done much better had the game been played later in the season. And Celtic, with manager Jock Stein absent through injury in a car crash, were rebuilding their side and really living on borrowed time.

Nevertheless, Rangers were consistent and they are a much better and certainly much more skilful side than their enemies allege. Certainly the Premier League in its first season was a success and developed into a thrilling race in early February when a five-point gap suddenly appeared among the leading quartet, Celtic, Rangers, Motherwell and Hibs, and the rest of the field. Even in April Celtic were still on top. But Rangers persisted – and won well.

Special mention must be made of Jock Wallace, whose built-in will-to-win, dynamic driving power and sheer force of personality have made him one of the truly great managers. Without that big man, his eyes fixed relentlessly on a particular goal, Rangers wouldn't have won the treble of Premier League, Scottish Cup and League Cup.

One target at a time, one game at a time – that is Wallace's attitude. And his final aim was 'a personal best of 27 games without defeat.' Said Jock: 'When we won the cup two years ago, we made it 26 matches without defeat. My aim was to beat that.' Rangers did, with 27 games undefeated. Added Jock: 'That's what this game of football is about, having targets and hitting them.'

Curiously, one reason for Rangers winning the football championship of Scotland

their breezy manager. Peter McCloy regained his place in goal and was magnificent again all season. Alex Miller established himself at back at last, while Colin Jackson and Tom Forsyth became the best defensive partnership in the country. John Greig was an inspiring captain, Johnny Hamilton provided accurate passes and Alex MacDonald reached the heights. Wee Tommy McLean was the artist, Bobby McKean the buzz-bomb.

Derek Johnstone, according to manager Wallace, the best player in Britain, got the goals and young Martin Henderson gave punch to the attack. On the bench were internationals Sandy Jardine and Derek Parlane, which proved that the club is greater than self.

'We've done it!' Manager Wallace and skipper John Greig are in ecstasy after Rangers won the Premier League title at Tannadice.

Derek Johnstone, who scored the goal which brought the championship to Ibrox, celebrates with a glass of champagne.

The Rangers spirit. Attack was the Ibrox motto and here defender Colin Jackson and centre-forward Martin Henderson are both up in an assault on the St Johnstone goal.

for the 36th time was a change in Wallace's training methods. After Rangers had lost five league games out of nine and had also crashed out of the European Cup, the manager decided relaxation should take the place of fierce training. So the players did hard physical training only on two mornings a week, the remainder of the time being spent working in small groups on individual skills.

Said Wallace: 'It's hopeless trying to work on an individual with 30 or so other players hanging around, so what we did was

tell certain players, never more than half a dozen, to report for ball-control practice while the rest have a day off.'

The manager felt the fact that Rangers could field a settled team for most of the season was a vital factor in the treble triumph. But Rangers also has the right blend – rare artists, determined defenders, a fine mixture of speed and subtlety.

It took Rangers a decade to get back on top in Scotland – but they did it in style. And once again they are the Scots Guards of football in this country. Once again boys dream of joining the most elite corps – the Ibrox brigade. Once again Rangers are the glamour club of Scottish soccer, 'Royal' Rangers, the side with the most dedicated fans of all, fans who will follow their team to the ends of the earth.

Argument rages, of course, as to whether the present Rangers eleven are as good as the famous outfits of the past. We veterans have marvelled at the skill of Alan Morton, David Meiklejohn, Bob McPhail, Willie subtle ball artist than Tommy McLean.

And Rangers still have players who have that Ibrox spirit which never dies – Tom Forsyth in particular. The former Motherwell sweeper plays with all the courage,

It was jubilation for Rangers – but dejection for Celtic. A home defeat by Ayr United put Celtic, who had fought so bravely all season, out of the title race and disappointment is written all over the faces of their players as they leave Parkhead after losing to Ayr.

Waddell, Torry Gillick, Willie Thornton and scores more; and, in the rosy glow of retrospect, it seems now that they were far superior to any players on the current scene. But that is unfair to the Rangers who play today.

For instance, Rangers have never had a more inspiring captain than John Greig, rightly chosen as Scotland's Player of the Year for season 1975–6, a more menacing attacker than Derek Johnstone, a more

determination and dedication of any Ibrox giant of the past – but he has skill, too, and has earned a place in the Scotland side.

Yes, Rangers are back in their blue heaven.

And what a night of joy, nostalgia, comedy and cheers they had when the club celebrated the grand slam with a gala occasion, including a match between the treble winning team of 1948–9 and the all-conquering lads of 1963–4.

But while Rangers just loved the new Premier League, not everyone else thought it was a big improvement on the old set-up. One of the troubles, said its critics, was that there was a shortage of goals. The Premier League produced an average of 2.78 goals a game, compared with an average of 3.10 in the previous year's First Division.

13

The year's most unlikely-looking team of stars. No wonder Hugh Taylor, linesman for a night, looks worried as he surveys this team at Ibrox. But they were all great players in their day – Ian McColl, Willie Woodburn, Sammy Cox, Willie Findlay, Willie Thornton, Eddie Rutherford, Jimmy Duncanson and Jimmy Smith. This old Rangers team were taking part in the celebrations at Ibrox when the side of season 1975–76 won the treble.

That meant a loss of around 57 League goals on the season.

Away goals dropped in the second half of the season to fewer than one per game, with the result that the percentage of home wins increased to 52 per cent over the season.

Away wins dropped slightly to 27 per cent and fell sharply to 21 per cent. And of the 38 Premier League matches which finished all square, nine were no-score draws.

The previous season, the top four clubs all averaged at least two goals a game. Last season only Celtic, who finished second, came close to that with 71 from their 36 games. Rangers' tally of 60 was the lowest for Scottish champions for 25 years.

St Johnstone, the bottom club, failed to find the net in six hours of football against Hearts as well as in 17 of their 36 matches. Hearts and Aberdeen didn't score in 11 games.

A note to pools punters. The score of Celtic 2, Dundee United 1, was the only score which was repeated in the 90 fixtures. And only 38 of the 90 fixtures ended with the same result the second time around.

Celtic and Ayr United scored 24 goals in their four meetings, with Celtic getting 12 of their 16 at Somerset Park.

Ironically, the relegation roulette wheel finally stopped opposite Dundee – because Dens Park saw more League goals (57) than any other ground.

Coincidence – Dundee, top of the Premier League after the opening game in August, were not only unlucky to go down on goal difference . . . for only once before has a Scottish club been relegated with as many as Dundee's total of 32 – and that was Dundee in 1938.

For most fans, however, the Premier League was a big success – more competitive, fiercer. And it could be even better this season.

SECRETS OF THE STRIKERS

Centre-forward used to be the glamour position. Every boy fancied himself as a new Hughie Gallacher, Jimmy McGrory or Willie Thornton and it was his dream to score the winning goal for Scotland against England. Mind you, there was little art about centre-forward play in the 1920s and 30s. It seemed crudely simple. You kicked the ball – kicked it hard, of course – and there was a goal.

Centre-forward, indeed, was the position occupied by a man who had to be a notable individualist, whose main task was to batter his way to supremacy. Of course, there were a few other types, leaders with more science than brawn, men like Thornton and Willie Bauld, jack-o'-lanterns who confused their opponents by unexpected sorties. On the whole, however, the job of the centre-forward was to score goals and most of the leaders did, because it was much easier then to put the ball in the net than it is now.

Today, though, few lads want to be strikers as centre-forwards are now called. For there is little glamour about the position. Strikers are the players most dourly and efficiently marked and goals by the men wearing the No. 8 or No. 9 jerseys are won mainly by brawn, extreme bravery or luck. Often, the job of the striker is to lay the ball off for an advancing full-back or mid-field player – so much has our game changed.

Goals seem to me to be becoming scarcer in modern football, hence the most plaintive appeal by the fans: 'All we are asking is give us a goal.'

In such short supply are goals that the back four, that fine old football institution wherein dwell the hearts of oak and legs of swift and sturdy resistance, have been asked in many cases to help to end the shortage their efficiency has done so much to create. Many clubs have ordered more and more defenders to go into the firing line, which shows that the need for goals is being discussed more urgently than ever.

Other solutions are a suggested 10 points for a win, five for a draw and an extra point per goal and a newspaper offer of £10 000 to the first player to score 30 goals in the English First Division.

In the end, however, the much-maligned, much-harassed, much-battered striker is still the man most likely to score goals.

Unlike so many old-time centre-forwards, the modern striker doesn't have to be a towering athlete with coal-heaver's shoulder's. Many are small – but tenacious. And that is the striker's philosophy – tenacity is all.

Says John 'Dixie' Deans, of Celtic: 'Few modern strikers have pretensions of being cultured footballers. I haven't. My job is to worry a defence, to win as many balls as I can and to stick away as many as possible of the chances that come my way.

'It's getting more difficult to score goals. The striker is being more tightly marked and you aren't given space. But there's no point in moaning. You've got to try to make room for yourself and also make the most of the fewer chances that are likely to come your way.'

15

Deans is noted for his ability in the air. How does he outjump taller opponents so often? He says there's no secret.

'It's not an aspect of my game that I've consciously developed. I've always had the knack of winning high balls. I put extra work in, of course, on jumping for high balls.'

If Deans is superb, for a smallish lad, when it comes to heading, few strikers can match Joe Harper of Hibernian for tucking the ball away in the adroit manner of the greatest of all, West Germany's Gerd Muller.

'Muller is the only player with whom I can identify,' says Harper. 'We've both got the same short, stocky build and similar styles of play. I think, like Muller, I can anticipate things inside the box and regularly stick one in the net.'

A brilliant goal scored by striker Willie Pettigrew of Motherwell against Celtic.

The reward of hard work. Celtic's Dixie Deans shows his joy after completing a hat-trick against Hibernian.

And many experts have commented on the way Harper can score goals out of nothing, turning as Jimmy Greaves and Lawrie Reilly used to do and getting in shots with either foot in tight areas, punching his shots without need of a big backswing.

To hit form, according to Harper, he needs a special type of training. 'I have to be quick over 10 or 15 yards and if I don't concentrate on short sprints I tend to become overweight and sluggish.'

His secret? It's the speed with which Joe sizes up situations. And Harper adds: 'I get most of my goals through just edging in front of defenders to get a touch of balls driven in from the flanks. But the ability to score goals is a gift really . . . you never lose it.'

Strikers must have that goal urge. Derek Parlane of Rangers certainly has. So keen is he to see the ball in the back of the Motherwell net that he tries to push it in with his hand.

Harper sometimes becomes annoyed with people who feel he doesn't work hard enough. 'I work harder than most fans think,' he declares. 'Admittedly when I lose the ball, I don't exactly burst a gut trying to win it back, but that's because I've used up a lot of energy in taking the ball through in the first place. I generally lose four or

five pounds during a game, which must prove something.'

The strikers' problem which worries Derek Parlane, of Rangers, is the fact that most have lean spells when goals seem as hard to come by as applause from the fans.

Like the other strikers, Parlane feels forwards are being marked tighter than they've ever been. 'The first thing I noticed in the new Premier League,' he says, 'is that strikers are being given the Italian treatment. You can hardly breathe because of opponents leaning on you. So I try to lay the ball off more. After all, the chances are not coming up now as easily as they did before the Premier League came into being.

'Another thing which worries a striker not scoring goals is frustration. You are liable to get into the referee's black book because of annoyance with yourself. You have to learn to control yourself.'

There is one aspect of the tighter marking which few people think about – but Willie Pettigrew, of Motherwell, does. He says: 'I did not expect goals to come easily in the Premier League, one reason being that opponents get to know more about your particular strengths and weaknesses by playing against you so often. I also think some clubs have placed greater emphasis on defence.

'But the fact that life has been made more difficult for me has forced me to work harder at improving my overall play. Getting fewer chances means I've had to concentrate to create more for myself.'

Pettigrew's secret? He's a goals-machine, a natural scorer, one of those instinctive players who will hit the ball at goal on the turn in situations where most other players would first want to stop the ball and look up to see what's on – and he's mobile.

Adds Pettigrew. 'I have to learn to be more philosophical.' He tends to lose confidence if he goes too many matches without scoring.

If you want to be a successful striker, you should take a crash course in psychology. That's the suggestion of Scotland's Ted McDougall, of Norwich City, who says:

'After our humiliation by England at Wembley, I was down in the dumps. But I had a chance discussion with Charlie Cooke at our headquarters before the Wembley match and that changed my life.

'Charlie was discussing the effect that reading books on single-mindedness had on his life. He was so enthusiastic that I hung on to his every word.

'I was contracted to play for five weeks in South Africa during the close season and that is one country short on entertainment

at night. They didn't even have television. I went out, then, loaded with the books Charlie Cooke had recommended and gave myself a crash course in psychology. I can tell you these weeks changed my life on and off the football field. Basically, my new philosophy on life revolves around the idea that I shouldn't worry about things which

One of the most resolute strikers in Scotland has been Eddie Morrison, of Kilmarnock and Morton. His secret: 'Hard work and graft,' he says.

are beyond my control, and as far as football is concerned I don't have to worry about spells without scoring or critical reaction from the fans.

'I simply concentrate on turning in worry-free displays and the goal touch follows naturally. Also, positive thinking helped me settle my internal dispute with Norwich for I fell in with my bosses' thinking and got down to hard work.'

The opponent Dixie Deans says gives him most trouble is the veteran Doug Smith, of Dundee United. 'A wonderful defender,' says Dixie. Here you see why Dixie feels that way about Doug. The United man wins a tackle with the Celt.

Undoubtedly McDougall will agree with Ian St John, that great Scottish player now a manager with Portsmouth, when he says:

'It annoys me when people criticize goalscorers for not having good ball control, artistry, and things like that.

'Some managers and coaches say players like McDougall and Deans and other strikers can't play. But when they get the ball in the penalty area, you know where it's going to go, don't you? You don't expect great strikers to be great footballers. You just say to a good striker, "Right, you just put the ball in the net, son," and he'll do it.'

That, in fact, is all we ask of the modern striker.

Yet the modern striker needs to be philosophic in this day of stern defence – or else he'll worry himself to death.

ONLY A DREAM FOR HEARTS
Rangers win the Scottish Cup Final

Donald Ford did his best to keep up the spirits of Hearts and their loyal supporters. The lively centre-forward, who had just left Tynecastle after a distinguished career, encouraged his friends with golden words.

Certainly Hearts needed something to pep them. For there were few teams who had gone into a Scottish Cup Final with such a dark cloud of pessimism hanging over them. No one outside the capital gave them a chance. The big question elsewhere seemed to be not so much if Rangers would justify their position as hot favourites to win the trophy – but how many goals they would win by!

Hearts, it appeared, needed a miracle. But Ford, one of the most respected professional footballers in the country, felt fairytales could still come true and he became the pundit the Hearts supporters liked most to listen to. Donald was, indeed just about the only forecaster who saw Hearts in with a chance.

'Hearts,' he said, 'are not by any means a great team. But they have a basic belief that they are not going to lose the final.' Donald had, he admitted, a great respect for Rangers. 'They have really blossomed,' he said, 'and they are so strong all-round that they could well dominate Scottish football in the way Celtic did between 1966 and 1974.'

How, then, did he think Rangers would lose to Hearts? Ah, went on Donald, while Rangers may be good, they had weaknesses all right. According to Donald, they lacked pace in centre defence and the backs played too wide.

Anyhow, he concluded, 'A cup final is a game on its own. Completely unpredictable. Don't write off Hearts.'

Was Donald whistling in the dark?

Practically everyone else considered the Tynecastle task was a Mission Impossible. It was Hearts' biggest challenge for years – and they were hardly in peak form. Also – Rangers had won the Scottish Cup 20 times. Hearts, who had spent most of the season near the bottom of the Premier League and who had struggled to reach the final, had won it five times.

Hope, however, sprang briskly in the hearts of the thousands of Tynecastle followers who made their way to a rather damp Hampden on the Saturday afternoon of 1 May 1976. Although Rangers were still strong favourites, the match had captured the imagination of the fans and there was a big crowd of 85 250 to see the teams line up like this:

HEARTS: Cruickshank, Brown, Burrell, Jefferies, Gallacher, Kay, Gibson, Busby, Shaw, Callachan, Prentice. Subs: Aird, Park.

RANGERS: McCloy, Miller, Greig, Forsyth, Jackson, MacDonald, McKean, Hamilton, Henderson, McLean, Johnstone. Subs: Jardine, Parlane.

REFEREE: R. H. Davidson, Airdrie.

Hearts' optimism lasted exactly 42 seconds. Astonishingly, it was Derek Johnstone, whose goal in 22 seconds had won the Premier League championship the previous week for Rangers, who sent his team on the way to victory in that time.

What a killer goal it was! And how deadly master marksman Johnstone showed himself to be. Hearts couldn't believe it. It was one of the swiftest goals in cup final history. From the kick-off, Rangers darted upfield. Johnstone was fouled by Jefferies. McLean took his usual accurate free-kick and before flabbergasted Hearts knew what was happening Johnstone had headed magnificently into the net, with the hapless Tynecastle defence rooted to the spot.

Hearts didn't know what had hit them. And eight minutes later it should have been all over but this time Johnny Hamilton missed an open goal.

Hearts, though, are a proud team. Skipper Jim Brown rallied his men. Brown began to raid on the right. The bewildered Edinburgh side hit back.

Hearts had a chance when Brown crossed and Prentice had the goal at his mercy, only to shoot past.

But Rangers, in command, knew they just couldn't lose after that remarkable start. Hearts had yet another amazing let-off when a bad pass back by Roy Kay allowed Martin Henderson to take the ball past the onrushing Cruickshank. The young striker cut the ball back to Johnstone but Jefferies barged in to clear the ball off the Ranger's toes.

Next, Rangers fans shouted abuse when Bobby McKean had the ball in the net again – only for the goal to be chalked off for offside.

Hearts never gave up – but they weren't powerful enough to upset the surging, confident Rangers. And right on the interval, Rangers, who had missed so many chances, got a second goal. A McLean corner was turned out to the edge of the penalty box. Alex MacDonald was lurking there. He saw his chance and took it and beat Cruickshank with a fine low shot.

It was a different and a better Hearts who turned out for the second half. They had winger Kenny Aird, whose omission had been a mystery to many, in for Sandy Burrell and what a difference the brilliant little Aird made.

He set his team off at a tremendous pace and Rangers had two escapes in five minutes. First, tall Peter McCloy made a significant full-length save from a crackling Drew Busby drive and then John Greig kicked off the line from John Gallacher. Shortly afterwards, the Rangers captain was injured by his own goalkeeper as McCloy was forced to dive at the feet of Willie Gibson.

It became a half bubbling with excitement. Cruickshank saved stylishly from McKean . . . a MacDonald shot trickled past the post with Cruickshank stranded. . . . Hearts changed the picture with fierce attacks. The fans loved it.

In a bid to earn glory, Hearts sent on their second substitute, Donald Park, who replaced Gibson, and, with 25 minutes left, Rangers put on Sandy Jardine in place of Hamilton.

Thrills still came. Hearts almost grabbed a goal when a McCloy clearance rebounded off Drew Busby, just inches wide of the post. At the other end, a McKean drive bounced off the bar.

Hearts were valiant. Hearts played with style and venom. Still, it was Rangers who held the edge. And then came the goal that really clinched the final.

McKean dribbled superbly down the right, beat Brown and brilliantly crossed. And there was Johnstone to smash the ball home from close range.

Hot action in the Scottish Cup Final as Hearts' Jim Brown tries to stop Rangers' Derek Johnstone, the man with the killer shot.

Hearts got their consolation a minute later, the 82nd.

An Aird cross was deflected to Graham Shaw, who simply had to tap the ball into an empty net. Hearts went down fighting. In the last minute Shaw headed against the Rangers bar.

But the match finished with Hampden erupting in a sea of red, white and blue as Rangers fans saluted a fine victory.

So there was no fairytale ending for Hearts. But they hadn't let Edinburgh down. Perhaps Rangers should have won by more goals but Hearts raided often enough and kept interest alive right to the end.

And Hearts, who became Scotland's representatives in the European Cup-winners Cup, revealed promise for the future, with Ralph Callachan showing he has the skill and temperament to make him one of Scotland's outstanding midfield players and Graham Shaw, signed for £20 000 from Dunfermline not long before the final playing his best game for his new club.

THE GOLDEN DAYS OF JIMMY DELANEY
Superstar without a Trace of Tantrums

Personality players, the men with the touch of magic, have been both football's lifeblood and its problem boys since the game was invented. And Scotland has supplied more than a fair share of that brash band of soccer extroverts who have been the idols of the fans and the despair of the managers.

While the terracings love the stars who compose the small, unusually talented, maverick minority, the bosses prefer the huge and disciplined majority of players, which is why soccer can be so dull nowadays.

Nevertheless, you can sympathize with the officials who have had to deal with the George Bests and George Connellys, gifted eccentrics who couldn't settle to the tough routine that is the background to all soccer fame.

It seems strange, however, that in these days of depth psychology and the wide dissemination of psychoanalytical ideas, we should be no nearer to coping with the problem of the unpredictable player than in the cloth cap and muffler days of between the wars. For we must realize that our football has always had its problem lads and has never been much good at dealing with them.

An exception was Arsenal manager Herbert Chapman, who found a solution to the problems of his greatest star, Alex James, the wee Scot with the big grin, the blob of a snub nose and the long shorts. Alex, as he told me himself, could provide trouble as well as superb entertainment on the field. But when he tried to start a 'rebellion' at Highbury, Chapman sent him for a long cruise – on a tramp steamer. Alex came back a more dedicated footballer than he had been.

It is said that it's harder today to be a professional football star than ever it was between the wars, with sudden wealth bringing fearful social dislocation and worries caused by a new situation for which nothing in his background has equipped a raw laddie.

I'm not so sure. It was just as difficult for the players like James, Jackson, Gallacher and scores more to adjust to stardom with top English clubs in the old days as it is now for players earning so much more.

And while many personality players make headlines because of extravaganzas on and off the field we must never forget that there were real superstars, men of extraordinary talents, who were as dedicated as any dour method pawn but who never kicked over the traces, were model club players as well as superb artists and made headlines only by their brilliant play on the field.

Such a one was Jimmy Delaney, dynamic individualist, a world class winger, worshipped by the fans, yet one of the truly great club-men.

How I wish we had today a waspish winger like Jimmy, the quiet little man who brought colour and glamour to football, who fought injury to reach the top.

Delaney made history by becoming the only player to win three cup-winners' medals in different countries – Scotland, England and Northern Ireland – but his own story is a mixture of glory and gloom.

It all began for Jimmy away back in 1933 when he joined Celtic. His play with Stoneyburn, his local team, had been watched by that shrewdest of scouts, Steve Callaghan, and manager Willie Maley – a boss, incidentally, who never had any trouble with big-headed or bizarre players because he sorted them out with eagle eye and blistering tongue before they could do the club or themselves any damage – was quick to sign him.

In his 13 years at Parkhead, Jimmy became a legend, all the more incredible because, in that era, Parkhead was an Aladdin's cave of soccer jewellery, with wizards like McGrory, Buchan, Crum, Paterson, Lyon and MacDonald in the team.

Delaney, however, was special, a darting imp with incredible speed, fine ball control and the heart of a lion.

His happiest day at Parkhead was in 1937 when Celtic beat Aberdeen in the Scottish Cup Final. Jimmy, at 24, won his first medal before a record crowd of 146 000.

The game he remembers best was the final of the Exhibition Cup in 1938 – staged at Ibrox – when Celtic won in extra time. 'This must have been one of the best games of all time, packed with action and end-to-end play,' he said.

It wasn't all glory for Jimmy, though, because injury and Delaney walked hand in hand. And at one time it looked as though he might never have a career to boast about, far less international recognition (14 caps, harder to come by in those days than now) and a splendid collection of medals and badges. Between the years 1939 and 1941, Jimmy had a broken left arm set three times.

Delaney's woes began at Gayfield Park, Arbroath, when he went up for a high ball, lost his balance and fell awkwardly. He took one of the nastiest arm breaks any football player has known.

The doctors told him the bones were broken so many times that they resembled a jigsaw puzzle.

There followed two agonizing years for Delaney. He was never far away from a hospital and at one time he was told his arm would have to be amputated. 'My happiest moment outside football was the day the doctor told me he had saved my arm,' said Jimmy.

The susceptibility to injury of 'Old Brittle Bones' – the newspapers' name for Delaney – provided acute worry for the SFA because no-one would insure the Celtic winger against injury, so it seemed he was all washed up as a Scotland player. But Jimmy was so popular that hundreds of his admirers thronged the street outside the SFA offices, then in Carlton Place, Glasgow, chanting: 'Delaney for Scotland.' They wanted their hero in the Scotland team, insurance or no insurance.

The man who saved the day for Jimmy was an old colleague of mine on the *Glasgow Evening News*, the respected sportswriter Harry Miller, who believed Delaney to be probably the greatest winger of all time.

When the SFA refused to take action, Harry found a friend in the insurance business who consented to insure Delaney.

It was well worthwhile because Jimmy Delaney became as famous as Bruce or Wallace when he gave Scotland victory at last over the auld enemy, England, by scoring the winning goal at Hampden in 1946 – and ending the most disastrous international saga Scotland had known, a series of dreadful defeats in the war-time internationals.

The year 1946 marked the end of a chap-

Even when he was more than 40, Jimmy Delaney, star with Celtic, Manchester United and Aberdeen, was still a master. Here he is when a member of the Elgin City side, taking part in a Scottish North Cup-tie against Aberdeen University. Young Innes, his University opponent at back, hadn't been born when Delaney starred for Celtic.

ter in the Delaney story – his farewell to Parkhead. He was transferred to Manchester United – for a fee of £4000.

In a way, Delaney was sorry to go, for big ideas started to permeate the Scottish scene. One suggestion was a super-league, which has now really happened with the formation of our Premier League.

In 1946, however, not everyone was in favour – certainly not the famous Celtic

historian, Dr James E. Handley, who wrote so entertainingly:

'Dazzled by the post-war boom in attendances and borrowing their notions from Hollywood, a few starry-eyed visionaries among the members of the directorates conceived the idea of a super-league. The Scottish League was to be wound up and a new League system would take its place. Under the plan, the terms First and Second Division would disappear, the new League being entirely on its own and having nothing to do with what the smaller clubs might decide.

'In the new Scottish National League there would be no terms of promotion or

What a team! This is the Celtic League Championship side of 1937–38 in which Jimmy Delaney was a star. Back row – Geatons, Hogg, Kennaway, Morrison, Crum, Paterson. Front row – Delaney, McDonald, Lyon, Divers, Murphy.

relegation, but for the four leading clubs at the end of the season there would be handsome cash prizes. Its representatives claimed they had three objects in view, improvement of conditions for players, raising of the standard of play and the provision of comfort for spectators. There would be a guarantee of £250 for visiting clubs, compared with the £100 of the pre-war League.

'Another idea was to make conditions so good that there would be no advantage in going to England. The new Scottish National League was to consist of 12 clubs: Aberdeen, Celtic, Clyde, Dundee, Falkirk, Hearts, Hibernian, Motherwell, Partick Thistle, Queen's Park, Rangers and Third Lanark. But Ayr United, Kilmarnock, Morton and St Mirren were invited to join if they felt that they could assume the heavy financial responsibilities involved.'

'After weeks of agitation, however, the smaller clubs successfully blocked the ambitious schemes of the more powerful ones and it was agreed that the A and B Division clubs of the period would accept a resolution to continue on the old lines, with automatic promotion and relegation, and some changes were made in the composition of the divisions.

'Of the grandiose scheme for spectacular soccer nothing further was heard.'

Incidentally, in 1946, there was a revolt by the fans. In a League match at Park-head against Rangers, Celtic raised their stand prices to – seven shillings and six-pence! So, many fans boycotted the game, and there was an attendance of only 30 000.

As Delaney, although rather old, in his thirties, to be called a Busby Babe, moved to England, the style of football in Scotland was changing. The innovation of the League Cup intensified the competition that the League and the Scottish Cup supplied. Success in it meant much to clubs and players and competition was such that the style of football changed.

Play was speedier with plenty of effort and running about but in skilful forward action – the sustained movement, the shrewd pass, the accurate finishing – there was a decline from the old standards. Goals and thrills took the place of polished adroit-ness and of triangular strategy there was hardly any.

As I said at the time. 'It is no longer fashionable to hold the ball and make posi-tion, no longer fashionable to be up for the return pass. You can do that now and again but not too often, please. Get it away!'

But in England Delaney was still making a hit – because there was football in his soul and he put the accent on ball play. He was just as big a favourite at Manchester as he had been at Parkhead and two years after joining Matt Busby he was the mainspring of United's FA Cup final victory over Blackpool. United won 4–2 after being twice behind.

Talking about his second cup-winners' medal, Jimmy said: 'I think we deserved to win the English cup. You see, we met only First Division teams all the way to the final – and we never played at home!'

United had to take the field that season at Maine Road, ground of their Manchester rivals, City, because Old Trafford had been severely damaged during the war.

Delaney's soccer safari was by no means over when he left Manchester United. In 1951 he joined Aberdeen and then played for Falkirk.

He was still on the glory trail and when he played with Northern Ireland club, Derry City, alas, out of existence now because of the troubles there, he received his third medal in 1954 when they won the Irish Cup.

His amazing sequence came to an end in 1955 when he was going for the grand slam. Although his new club, Cork, reached the final of the Eire Cup, they were defeated 3–2, after being two goals up.

Jimmy also played with Elgin City, and,

after leaving football, he was employed in a steel plant.

Delaney, although a world class star, had none of the tantrums of other brilliant footballing personalities. He was a model professional – and he never had a bad word for anyone.

The greatest player he ever saw? Stanley Matthews. The best manager? Sir Matt Busby, of Manchester United, 'the master of them all', according to Jimmy. We can truthfully say that Jimmy Delaney was also a master of football in every way.

HERESY...brings spice to the Scottish Soccer Scene

Football, especially in Scotland, can be the most conservative of sports, hidebound by tradition. Change is frowned on. New ideas aren't welcomed.

So heresy is a bad word in Scottish soccer. Too many people forget that free personal choice now sounds splendid and inspiring and feel it should be hated and hunted. The word heresy still conjures up in parochial Caledonian circles the smell of people burning at the stake.

But to be a heretic today is almost a human obligation for, after all, the gist of heresy is free personal choice in act and thought and the rejection of traditional faiths and customs. Sometimes heresy ceases to be dangerous and becomes desirable.

And Scottish football has always had its heretics – and their views make joyous reading.

Here are some of the modern 'heretics', whose ideas are worthy of consideration . . .

GET RID OF THE HAMPDEN ROAR!

It's the most famous sound in football – The Hampden Roar – as loud as a Wagnerian chorus, as fierce as a wolf pack, as intimidating as the pounding of a cavalry charge, the most fearsome noise in all sport.

We're rather proud of it, we Scots, and we like to think that when the overtures to the tremendous orchestration of sound that is the Roar rises into the pale Mount Florida sky the English tremble and foreign footballers bite their nails.

It would be a brave man, then, who stands up to declaim that the Hampden Roar probably does more harm than good. But Sandy Jardine, of Scotland and Rangers, is a bold lad as well as a world class footballer. And there's sense in what he says about the Hampden Roar.

'Our Scottish fans are the best in the world,' according to the Ranger, 'but often the Hampden Roar spoils our pattern.' Heresy? Sandy could be right.

After all, Scotland's results at Hampden are unpredictable. And not only Sandy Jardine feels it is the supporters' craving for action which produces an atmosphere in which it is difficult for the Scotland team to play constructively.

Too many Scottish fans still don't realize how much football has changed. Patience is now the main virtue.

Yet British crowds still howl for red-hot aggression and boo players who try to slow play. Alas, the need for modern teams to probe for openings, to try and pick the lock of an opposing defence rather than blast a hole through the door, is rarely appreciated by spectators in Northern Hemisphere countries.

Says Kilmarnock manager Willie Fernie, whose brilliant side blends the old with the new better than most in Britain. 'The great teams of today are renowned for the way they build attacking moves constructively, from deep position.

'There is little sense in repeatedly bashing speculative balls up the field for players

A magic moment in the life of Sandy Jardine as he captains Scotland in the match at Hampden against East Germany.

to chase. But very often they are pressurized into playing that way by their supporters.'

Too many spectators don't realize, in fact, that it is impossible for any team to keep bombing away forward for an entire 90 minutes. There must always be stages in a game where a team must try to take the steam out of opponents by knocking the ball about cleverly and forcing the other side to chase in vain after it.

Sandy Jardine, however, thinks that the problem of getting supporters to accept this type of football is particularly acute in Scotland. And so do I.

I agree with Sandy when he says that in international football players get behind the ball so quickly that it is essential at times to knock the ball back and forth across the park and wait for the other team to commit themselves.

Maybe, then Scotland would win more games at home if the lads on the terracing muted the Hampden Roar and allowed the players more time in which to grab the vital goals.

MOVE THE BOSSES OUT OF GLASGOW!

There were few better or more stylish backs than Bobby Ancell in the days before the

Bobby Ancell takes over as manager at Dundee. Not yesterday – as you realize when you look at the Dens Park players in this picture, including Bobby Seith, Alex Hamilton, Andy Penman, Charlie Cooke, Bobby Cox and Jim Easton.

war. And certainly there were no deeper thinkers about football than Mr Robert Ancell when he became a manager later on with Dunfermline Athletic, Motherwell and Dundee.

Always a believer in sweet, scientific soccer, Bobby Ancell achieved fame with his famous 'Ancell Babes' of Fir Park in the early 1960s and he was recognized as one of the outstanding football technicians of all time.

Although he is in semi-retirement after a distinguished career, Bobby still has the soccer world buzzing with his ideas. Once he maintained that Scottish football should be played in summer, with a break in winter.

'How,' he used to ask, 'can anyone play good football in mud, ice and snow, on surfaces which don't provide a footing? It's silly to me. You might as well ask an expert snooker player to do his stuff on a torn-up table.'

Now he believes the SFA should move their heaquarters out of Glasgow, to somewhere like Perth or Ayr. 'After all,' he says, 'the English League have their offices well away from the hub of the game, in quiet

Lytham St Annes. I think the SFA should move out of Glasgow to a more serene spot away from the established influences of the game.'

Undoubtedly there is a school of thought who believe football is ruled by the big Glasgow clubs – but what a howl there would be if the SFA moved away from Park Gardens in the city.

Bobby won't prove popular with the coaches of today who base their strategy on defence. 'There's far too much defensive play nowadays,' he says. 'And too much emphasis is put on drill and phrases like good work-rate. Indeed, we have too much coaching. Players are individuals who have temperaments and they ought to be encouraged to use their natural talents.

'The game has become far too theoretical and it's ridiculous to tie a gifted ball-player down to a defensive role.

'I wonder what these coaches would say to a Stanley Matthews or a Gordon Smith?

'My view is that there should be some reward for teams who play attacking football. Giving an extra point to teams who score more than three goals is worthy of consideration. The aim of the game is to score goals – not just to prevent the ball going into the net.'

Meanwhile, Bobby, like so many others, feels the Premier League has produced more competitive interest – but doesn't believe it has improved the general standard of the game.

He'd like to see a return to the old style when players were allowed to play the game as it should be played – off the cuff.

Many will agree with him when he says method madness is killing football, now more like a game of chess.

BRING BACK THE TRIANGLES!

A revival of the best of the old-time ideas – that's the solution to our football ills presented by the man who was by far the most successful of all Scotland team managers.

He is Malcolm Macdonald, undefeated in his temporary spell as this country's international boss as he saw his teams draw 1–1 with Wales, beat Ireland 2–1, defeat the English League 3–1 and hammer the Welsh Under–23s 6–0.

Like Jardine, like Ancell, Malcolm Macdonald puts scientific soccer above method. He was one of the most versatile players who ever wore a Celtic jersey – but even when he played at centre-half his motto was 'attack'.

As manager of Scotland, Kilmarnock and Brentford, he was prepared to give the players all the freedom they wanted.

'Football,' he told me, 'is mainly a game of triangles,' and he pointed out that when he played for Scotland – in the days when there was no team boss – no tactics were laid down.

'We used to get together for a day or two before the big match,' he reflected. 'We made ourselves into groups, the left-winger, inside-left and left-half, for example, and worked out the basic plans for set pieces.

'Then we talked about what we were going to do and worked in triangles. It was up to us to learn how to dovetail and find out our likes and dislikes on the field.'

Malcolm believes that football here will improve only when there are more good players. 'No matter what you do,' he insists, 'a team can only be as good as its players and the more good players in a side the better it will be.

'That sounds elementary but today too many coaches seem to think they are magicians and that they can make ordinary players into stars or, rather, star teams, by employing more and more drill and method.

Even further back in the Ancell history. This is Bobby in his playing days with Dundee in a game against Rangers at Hampden. Others in the picture are Gray and McKenzie, of Dundee, and Duncanson, of Rangers.

'To me, that's just not on. Football is about good players, just the same as athletics is about the best runners and hurdlers and golf is about the great superstars who score in the 60s.

'We still breed fine quality players in this country but, alas, not enough of them.'

Now Malcolm's job is seeking the kind of players he feels his first love, Celtic, want. And he puts the accent on clever inside-forwards and wing-halfs – 'although we don't call them that today, do we?

They're all-purpose men, I suppose.'

Malcolm thinks one trouble about the Scottish scene is that players are moulded into the system, instead of being allowed to exploit their talents and he added:

'In my time, if you were attacking, then your forwards were supported by two wing-halfs. If you were defending your defence was bolstered by two inside-forwards. The wing halfs and inside forwards were the hub of the team. If you had good players in these positions, you were made.'

But, in the opinion of Macdonald, who is fair and doesn't believe all the great things in football happened in the past, not only coaches are to blame for the changes in style.

Social conditions, he thinks, play their part. 'The boys of today don't spend all their waking hours playing football or thinking about the game as we used to do.

'When we joined a junior, never mind a senior, club we were expert in trapping, passing, shooting, heading — for we had practised these arts until it became dark.

'Now it's different. Young players going senior have to be taught the rudimentary arts — arts we learned at school or in the street.

'That's life, though. There are more things for the youngsters to do in this modern age.

'And we must realize — and certainly the men in the game must understand this — that football is not now the only recreation of Scotland's youth, the be-all and end-all of everything that it used to be in this country.'

BAXTER, LAW, JAMES, PELE, DI STEFANO, CRUYFF, BECKENBAUER, MORTON, BLOOMER - But Who Was The Perfect Player?

There will never, I'm afraid, be the perfect footballer. He remains a fantasy figure. You may say Pele, Best, Di Stefano, James and Baxter are entitled to the description. But someone is bound to say: 'Ah, but they were not 90-minute players' – which, in the gruesome modern soccer jargon, translates into: 'They could be faulted by lack of work-rate.'

The complete footballer would swoop like a hawk, soar like an eagle, play like a tiger for the whole match. He would dribble like Matthews, tackle like Dave Mackay, head like Jimmy McGrory, shoot with the ferocity of Tommy Gemell. He would be skilful, courageous, determined, powerful, quick. And he would have character, charisma, vision, loyalty. He would be utterly unselfish, but he would also be a king of individualists.

So you can see we will never find the perfect player.

That, however, doesn't stop us arguing about what is the asset most valuable in a footballer. Everyone has a different view.

Some experts, like Jock Stein of Celtic, aver that love of the game is the factor most common to greatness. 'Skill,' says the Parkhead boss, 'is an obvious requirement – but all the outstanding players have been in love with the game.' And among his great ones Stein lists Jim Baxter, Denis Law, Dave Mackay, Bobby Murdoch, Di Stefano, Pele, Bobby Charlton, Johnny Haynes, Jimmy Greaves, Rivelino, Cruyff and Puskas.

Adds Jock: 'They were all different but they all made things happen – and they all loved the game.'

While skill is mandatory, sheer ability isn't all if one is to become the perfect player. A school of thought believes that of all the elements that make up the chemistry of a sportsman that most compelling is will. Certainly a player will never succeed if he isn't driven by a burning desire to win.

High on the list of priorities is grafting. That's the view of England manager Don Revie whose demands are many and detailed. Don declares that ability itself is not enough. 'The great player adapts himself to the game as it unfolds. He thinks. He works. He is all for the team. He never stops grafting even when things are going wrong.'

Revie singles out that great Scot, Bobby Collins, of whom the England supremo says: 'Bobby kept on running, taking his man away, making it easier for others. Like all great players, he grafted on the bad days. When you add that to the magic of their skill you really have something.'

If you are to become the perfect player, you need something not often talked about – balance. And one who had it was the little man so many believed to have been even better than Stanley Matthews – the wee blue devil, Alan Morton.

Alan had perfect balance – and that made him a holy terror to England, whose selectors fielded man after man in an effort to solve what was actually an insoluble puzzle.

England even thought up one that was unique.

They tried the experiment of playing against him a half-back of Morton's own diminutive dimensions – poor Magee of West Bromwich Albion. But he proved as ineffective as those before and the others after him.

Morton may not have been the perfect footballer – but he was the complete winger. He had every trick and was a master in the art of ball control. It was near impossible, said his opponents, to divine his intentions, so effectively could Morton change his mind and his direction of travel in a split second.

A player who went near to being the perfect attacker if not the complete footballer was the legendary Steve Bloomer, and his story provides another example of one of the most fascinating aspects of football – you don't have to be a handsome athlete, an illustration for the cover of a health and strength magazine, to become a magnificent footballer.

You can be tall and skinny, small and tubby, gawky, gangling, delicate, but these are no drawbacks if you have skill.

Bloomer, for instance, was slight, pale-faced, indolent-looking and a more unlikely looking athlete one would scarce select as a famous footballer. As one reporter said so long ago: 'He is not the sort of man whose life any doctor would insure at sight.'

But he had the power to mesmerize goal-

Perfection, alas, has never yet been found in any footballer. So say the experts.

But we believe that many players of yesterday and today have ingredients which make them superb in many ways.

Can you imagine better and more inspiring captains in any walk of life than Rangers' John Greig and Celtic's Billy McNeill?

Can you recall a player who ever placed the ball more accurately than Tommy McLean, of Rangers?

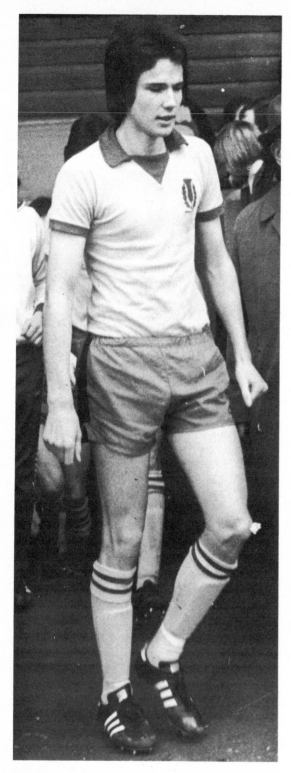

keepers and he was so obsessed with the grand idea of scoring goals that he is still reckoned among the top ten of English players.

Perhaps he was the greatest of all individualists. Because of Bloomer it was written: 'He does nothing like anyone else. That dash for the goal-line is a Bloomer dash; that single-handed dribble a Bloomer dribble; that fierce rattling shot is a Bloomer shot; that superb forward pass is a Bloomer pass; that glorious bid for victory in the eleventh hour is the consummation of Bloomer's art.'

Don't forget, however, what I said previously about will. They said, too, about Steve Bloomer: 'This triumph of the strong will, those ruling passions, have made Bloomer a great footballer. He is a destroying angel on the ball.'

The perfect footballer must be the perfect team-man – and it isn't always easy to synchronize with others. Anyhow, in Scotland, the true art of football was to blend players, to allow them to play naturally, whether skilfully or robustly.

We all have our favourite types. You may like the dashing striker or the dazzling winger. My pet player is the type who was once symbolic of the artistry of Scottish soccer. To him flair was all. The shrug of the shoulder, the flick of the hip, the dummy, the careful precision pass, the oily swerve – these were his weapons and how well he used them. He was usually an inside-forward and he was a specialist in altruism. His job was to make goals, not score them, to hold the ball for the fraction of a second needed for his younger and more virile colleagues to take up position,

Have you ever seen a young player who promised more than Partick Thistle defender, Alan Hansen?

What veteran ever did better or played more urgently than Bobby Watson, of Motherwell?

then slide the ball to the man most likely to be able to shoot without distraction. This type was an individualist, a master of the ball, and I loved him, whether Mason, James, Buchan, Walker, Williamson, Mills or McMillan.

But it took all kinds to make Scottish football great. There were rough players

Has there ever been a more versatile player than Derek Johnstone, of Rangers, who shows international skill both in attack, defence and mid-field?

All these players come near being perfect in their respective roles.

possessed every attribute.

Listen to Dave Mackay, manager of Derby and one of the greatest Scottish half-backs of all time:

'It is impossible to build total accomplishment into one frame. Skill is the major factor but some players have one thing going for them, others have something else.

'You must have enthusiasm, Colin Todd's balance, Billy Bremner's aggression. But how can anyone put it all together? Stanley Matthews was the greatest dribbler of all time but what could he do in the air? Nothing.

'John Charles was outstanding in that respect and he had a lot of other things going for him as well. He was versatile, too. Was he the perfect player? He went near, I suppose, but what would you really settle for? Best's explosive bursts, Law and Greaves in the box, Cliff Jones's pace, Bremner's spirit, Baxter's touches, Beckenbauer's passing?

'You would have a priceless player if you could put all these assets together in one man.'

Who's your fancy as the man nearest to being the complete player?

I'd go, I think, for Di Stefano, of South America and Real Madrid. He did everything. He attacked, he defended, he organized. Sir Matt Busby believes Di Stefano was the greatest ever.

And while Pele must take the crown for attacking prowess, Di Stefano wins the title for limitless all-round excellence.

He had the gift of skill and he knew what to do with it.

Until a new one comes along, Di Stefano will be my favourite.

and gentle players; there were saints and sinners.

Was there the perfect player in the old days? I don't think so. No-one has ever

43

FREE THE KIDS FROM THE ROBOT'S GRIP-Scotland should take a tip from Don Revie

It isn't often that Scots praise English football – but England manager Don Revie is carrying out a quiet revolution which should be followed north of the border.

It's a revolution at schoolboy level and it is certainly hailed with delight and admiration by me. Revie believes that only by allowing youngsters freedom of expression will Britain discover a Cruyff or a Pele or a Matthews or Smith to lead our World Cup challenge in the 1980s.

He has held a series of mass meetings to preach his theory for the future to the schools' soccer coaches. 'You teachers hold the future of football in your hands just as much as professional managers,' he tells them.

And the man who is one of the game's most brilliant thinkers, who has in his time practised all kinds of ideas, from an artistic individual style as a player to solid, systematic soccer as manager of Leeds United, makes a statement which should be printed in giant letters over every football ground: 'Don't fetter the kids with systems at an early age.'

He adds: 'Don't let them get too obsessed with winning trophies before their natural talent comes into full bloom.'

Like Revie, we in Scotland who believe in natural, exciting, skilful football and deplore the transistorized, soulless, method game which is the real reason for the decline in gates and interest, have good grounds for claiming that flair is far too precious to be stifled by inhibitions at an early age.

While the game, even at school level, must have a framework to give it some semblance of tidiness, it is far too early to drill into boys rigid systems such as 4–3–3 and 4–2–4.

As Revie says: 'If we want players of natural brilliance to emerge – players such as Pele – it is better to let the kids go out and enjoy their game, to take opponents on and beat them and go through and shoot at goal.

'Rigid formations at too early an age can suppress natural inclinations and natural talent blossoms best through doing what comes naturally.

'I know it is asking a lot of schoolmasters and some of the boys, perhaps, to put the enjoyment of uninhibited football before winning their town and city and county trophies. Even at ground level they like to win, to have honours to show for their footballing ability.

'But I feel sure the best thing is to allow natural flair to emerge in an unfettered way and then to leave the clubs to blend it and mould it into systems when the boys reach the age of 17 or so.'

Well, I suppose the modern game needs some kind of system – though I'm not so sure of that at times when I shudder at the drabness and monotony of some of the matches I watch. But football thrives on great players, exciting players, artistic players like Kenny Dalglish, Tommy McLean, Eddie Gray; players with flair, players who are not bound by convention, players who illuminate dull method like beacons.

It is true that in Scotland our teams, at

44

The stars who appeal to the Scottish football fans aren't those who deal in method play. They are stylish players like . . .

Alex O'Hara of Rangers

all levels, are not as rigidly drilled as they are in other countries but we still put far too much stress on method. Certainly boys should not be turned into school robots. They should not only be allowed but also

Drew Jarvie of Aberdeen

encouraged to display all the natural flair they possess.

The trouble with too much football nowadays is that Safety First is the motto. It is better, feel frightened managers, to draw than to lose, better to keep your own goal intact than to score. Keep the other side.

45

Kenny Aird, of Hearts

Johnny Graham of Ayr United

No wonder so much excitement and colour has gone out of football. Attack should be all in the game. After all, in the early days, the late 1860s, you would have seen seven forwards and four defenders disputing the field.

But the game became systemized. Soon one of the three centre-forwards was eliminated and a second full-back came into the order of battle. By 1883 the pioneers of Cambridge University removed the second centre-forward and played a third, or centre, half. Five forwards, three halves, two backs and a goalkeeper was the accepted line-up by the end of the century.

And that was the best formation, the most

Gordon Smith of Kilmarnock

Harry Hood of Celtic

flexible, the most attractive – and I may be old-fashioned but I believe a return to that way of playing would enliven and embellish a game which has grown weary and lack-lustre.

The alleged experts kept experimenting, however. We had the W-plan in attack and the general employment of the centre-half as a third full-back, glued to the centre-forward near the goal-mouth.

The years just before the end of the 19th century marked one of the greatest transitional periods in the history of football. The traditional, gentlemanly – and far tougher and rougher – football of the ex-public schoolboys was to disappear from the playing fields, being superseded by the subtleties and skills of the professional per-formers who valued their limbs as stock-in-trade and got their effects by cunning rather than the unquestioning zeal of those who modelled themselves on the Light Brigade.

The style changed, and the main feature was the eclipse of dribbling which, with brisk forcing of your way through, had been the way to play in the good old days when Lord Kinnaird was the star of the Old Etonian team.

The new style dictated that you played as a side and you had an understanding from pole to pole. But attack was the name of the game. It had style and grace, glamour, drama, excitement.

Why did it have to change? Fright – fear of losing. Football became big business and success was all . . . well, safety, rather, was all.

It wasn't until the great Hungarians who swept all before them in the 1950s came to Britain that we realized what we had been missing. Puskas and Company were hailed as a new breed of footballers. They weren't. They played football in the way the great masters had played in Scotland in the past.

Football here, as well as abroad, often looked like a finely rehearsed ballet danced by men with the brains of chess grand-masters. They wove fresh patterns and scorned the rigid tactical lines which had cast a blight on British teams.

The trouble with our football is that we now have no special style to offer the world. We head no particular school. The great acrobatic champions are the South Ameri-cans. The classic teams and players are to be found in countries such as Holland, Spain and West Germany. Thanks to method and fear of losing, we just play the sort of football which long, grinding seasons of the League game have brought about.

We need more men like Don Revie who will preach the gospel of freedom of ex-pression.

We do not, of course, want to go back to the bad old days when 'the football was a bloodie and murthering practice rather than a felowly sport or pastime'.

But we must put emphasis on attack. We must find players with the skills and per-sonality of a Gordon Smith, Alan Morton, Alex James, Tommy Walker, Billy Steel, Hughie Gallacher, Sammy Cox, Willie Bauld and the scores more who made foot-ball so fascinating.

We should listen to experts like Willie Henderson, that wonderful little winger who became a legend in the blue of Scotland and of Rangers, a player of the old school who lit up a soccer scene becoming drab with superb individual thrusts. Henderson told me:

'I hate football goemetry. You know what I mean – the game reduced to so many angles and theorems. There is far too much off-the-field theorizing in the modern game. I'm convinced pre-arranged strategies and theories can be overdone. General tactics, yes. You have to figure out in advance what sort of game to play as a team, how to cope with the opposition's strong points and so on.

'But I know that if I had to try to con-centrate on specific moves, moves designed for me individually, I'd never beat my man and get the ball across.'

The Italians, incidentally, can take much

of the blame for the defensive football which casts its blight over our football. They made defensive football pay off, for a spell anyhow. But in the end the dour men of Inter and the others choked the players' ability and eliminated all the natural beauty in the game.

As Josef Masopust, the famous Czechoslovakian player, said: 'Technique in football has not improved in recent years. And pre-war football was more attractive to the spectators than it is today. The trouble is that every player going on to the field has his exact orders and is thus limited.

So football now allows even technically not very skilled players to play perfectly their defensive roles. I feel that defensive tendencies have meant that football won't survive as a major sport for more than 40 years.

'I do not believe the problems of defensive football can be solved by any change of rules. Maybe making the goalmouth bigger would help because we need to score more goals if we are to keep the spectators happy.

'We also need better players and they must be trained from an early age.'

Which is why, I repeat, we need more idealists like Don Revie.

Catch them young – and we will find the stars to crack that dreadful 'catenaccio' defence.

KING JOHN OF HAMPDEN-Grieg's happiest day

In a long and illustrious career, studded with honours galore, one day stands out in the memory of Rangers captain John Greig as his happiest in football – the Saturday of 25 October 1975.

That was the afternoon John skippered his first League-Cup-winning side – and was chosen by manager Willie Ormond to play for Scotland against Denmark on the following Wednesday, *at the age of 33.*

There was no doubt, however, that Greig was King John, the League Cup supremo, in the match at Hampden which Rangers won 1–0 over their old rivals, Celtic.

Greig the mighty never faltered, never put a foot wrong, on a day when mistakes were frequent and nerves were stretched to breaking point.

Although he was listed as a left-back, he was all over the Rangers defence, marshalling them into a display that equalled anything ever presented by the famous Iron Curtain of George Young and Company.

It was, however, one of the strangest League Cup Finals in the history of the competition.

In a bid to prevent the trouble which so many believe is caused by whisky, cheap wine and cans of beer, the battle was scheduled to start at one o'clock, thus spoiling the lunch of the residents of the Mount Florida district, who quail at the destruction so often caused to their property by the Hampden legions.

The early kick-off proved a success in that there was little or no crowd trouble in the ground – and the 58 806 spectators who turned up became the real men of the day. The fans who had been criticized all season kept the game alive, trying to breathe badly-needed inspiration into the play, singing, cheering and encouraging non-stop.

The one o'clock start, though, didn't seem to suit the players, who were put out of their stride by the change in pattern, and the final never lived up to expectations.

There was only one goal in it and the teams were evenly balanced – but what a goal it was.

It came in 66 minutes – at 16 minutes past two – and so it deserves its own niche in history as surely the earliest goal ever scored in a cup final.

It was a MacDonald masterpiece – and how wee Alex MacDonald must have enjoyed scoring it, for it was the mid-field man who was blamed for allowing St Etienne, Rangers' European Cup opponents, to score a late goal in France on the Wednesday before, by making a mistake with a bad pass-back.

The goal came at a time when Celtic for once seemed to have the edge. Colin Stein relieved the pressure with a long lob. The bustling Derek Parlane stormed after it and won a duel with Celtic's Roddy MacDonald. The Ranger crossed. Johannes Edvaldssen headed away.

But only to the clever Quinton Young on the Ranger's left. Young might have tried to score himself. Instead, he intelligently headed across goal again.

MacDonald had read the situation brilliantly. As the ball came over he rocketed himself at it – and nodded a wonderful goal to give Rangers a win they narrowly deserved.

Apart from the goal, however, there was little to remember about the final. It was a match which ran away from the players, hurry-hurry-scurry all the time, with even accomplished artists like Tommy McLean

been fought between Glasgow's ancient rivals.

Too many of the tackles were, to put a fine point on it, 'over-enthusiastic'. The referee's book was out three times, to enter the names of Celtic's Harry Hood and Pat McCluskey and Rangers' Tom Forsyth. He took a lenient view of the proceedings for several others might have suffered.

Indeed, there was a storm after the game.

Rangers' captain John Greig with the League Cup.

and Ken Dalglish getting rid of the ball as if it were a hot potato.

Nobody wanted to be caught in possession. No wonder, perhaps, for this was also as tough a League Cup Final as has ever

As Rangers celebrated their first Scottish League Cup victory for five years, a row blew up over referee Bill Anderson's handling of the game and Celtic said they would protest about the bookings of their players.

Celtic, however, never struck their true form, although they had their moments, as when Tommy Callaghan hit the bar.

51

Rangers were more forceful than Celtic, more intent on attack, and thus, without producing their top form either, were entitled to take the League Cup.

It was hardly suprising that the final failed to thrill, for the League Cup is not the best of Scotland's tournaments. Not only are the early sectional games a distraction before the real cup-tie business begins, and the quarter-finals usually a yawn, but also the final comes at a bad time.

Only days before the finalists had been in hectic action in Europe and on the following Wednesday many of the players were in Scotland's blue against Denmark.

Rangers, for instance, had lost goalkeeper Peter McCloy – through a curious injury received at shooting-in practice in St Etienne just before the European Cup-tie – and both teams must have been tired after their trips abroad.

It is time for this part of the football calendar to be re-examined and the whole tournament re-vamped and used as a tonic in the dreary mid-winter weather.

The teams at Hampden were:

Rangers: Kennedy, Jardine, Greig, Forsyth, Jackson, MacDonald, McLean, Stein, Parlane, Johnstone, Young. Subs: Miller, McKean.

Celtic: Latchford, McGrain, Lynch, McCluskey, MacDonald, Edvaldssen, Hood, Dalglish, Wilson, Callaghan, Lennox. Subs: Glavin, McNamara.

Referee: W. Anderson, East Kilbride.

For Celtic, perhaps the hero was burly Icelander Johannes 'Shuggy' Edvaldssen, who has made such a hit at Parkhead. In a bright Celtic start, Edvaldssen seemed to pull a muscle as he tried to storm through. Play was held up for a long time as he received treatment. He limped for the rest of

A new Celtic favourite is Johannes 'Shuggy' Edvaldssen, the Icelandic star.

the game but was always trying to get Celtic into the attack.

Another Celtic star was the veteran Bobby Lennox, playing as well as ever, just as fast at 30-odd as he was in his teens, and a beautiful flick by Bobby early on gave Ken Dalglish a chance which, if it had been taken, might have turned the whole course of the game.

On the other hand, Colin Stein had the ball in the Celtic net, only for offside to have been given before.

The most controversial character in the curious final was undoubtedly Tom Forsyth, the Rangers sweeper. What a game the former Motherwell player, who had been dogged by injury, played for Rangers. There was little action of any kind that did not involve the Ibrox star.

He was on the scene at every booking, he hardly gave Ken Dalglish a kick at the ball, he was booed by the Celtic fans for hefty tackling. But big Tam swept serenely through the game and ended up with Greig in the top flight.

It was a sad day for Celtic, who, in modern times, have made the League Cup a monopoly. They have appeared in the past 12 finals, a stint started before anyone had heard of the Beatles or the pound became a dirty word in Europe.

Now Celtic and Rangers have each won the cup eight times. Incidentally, it was Celtic and Rangers who drew the biggest final gate in 1965, when 107 609 saw Celtic win 2–1.

But the days of the huge League Cup Final gates are over and, it must be repeated, this tournament could do with a different dressing – although Celtic can remain happy in the knowledge that practically one million spectators (actually 884 478) have watched them play in their 12 successive League Cup Finals, yet another memorable record in the fantastic Parkhead history.

THIS MAN McLEOD-Profile of Soccer's Cheerful Earful

You could always tell a football club manager in the good old days by his waistcoat, his watch-chain with a cup medal dangling from it, his bowler, and his refusal to communicate with the Press unless with a grunt or a 'Mind your own business.'

Although he seldom took part in training, he ruled his players with a rod of iron and the best most of his lads would say of him was: 'I'd swing for that so-and-so.'

Times have changed. Today's archetypal soccer boss is sleekly dressed, has a trendy hair style, talks to reporters like a professional public relations man, injects his personality and ideas into his players by training with them and, on the day of the match, he is, from his seat in the dug-out, just as much involved in the play as any of the men on the field.

The most flamboyant of the current crop of bright, brash brigadiers of football is Ally MacLeod, who is so beloved of his players that they say – and mean it – 'We'd die for the boss.'

No wonder. Fast talking MacLeod became the toast of Aberdeen last season. Not since Jock Stein swept into Parkhead and immediately guided his team to a Scottish Cup victory, had a new manager made such an immediate impact. And, in a few months, Ally MacLeod displaced North Sea oil as the great Aberdeen phenomenon. He turned, too, into the most confident cock o' the north the granite city had ever seen.

But that's Ally. Never at a loss for a word. A super enthusiast. An optimist. An extrovert. A passionate supporter of his own club.

And, despite unfounded allegations that he is Scotland's Brian Clough, he is one of the most likeable men in football.

He is adored by his players. Listen to young John McMaster, the Aberdeen midfield star, who had been expecting a free transfer until the arrival of MacLeod – and suddenly found he had become a keyman in the Dons' remarkable revival. Said John, a 20-year-old from Greenock who has a wonderful footballing future: 'It is the new boss's inimitable zest and enthusiasm for football that has been responsible for instilling in me a new confidence and ambition.

'When Mr MacLeod came along it was like starting a new life. He talks a lot – but that's what we need, for he knows football inside out. And he's fair to everyone. All the Aberdeen players would die for him.'

MacLeod was just the tonic Aberdeen needed when the fair-haired manager took over at Pittodrie after a ten-year stint with Ayr United, a club of part-timers with whom he had worked so many miracles that the Somerset Park side were feared by the giants.

Gloom surrounded Pittodrie. The once proud scarlet-clad Dons seemed doomed to relegation from the Premier League.

Almost at once, however, the irrepressible Ally got to work and inside weeks he was a folk hero, not only instilling new spirit into the team and bringing back the crowds to Pittodrie but establishing a remarkable rapport with the canny and kindly folks of the city and surrounding countryside.

Don't call him Mr Aberdeen, though. His

nickname in the north is Muhammad Ally – and the loudspeakers blare that record at Pittodrie as the manager walks along the track to the dug-out, where his antics can be an entertainment, so involved does he become in the game.

Now, just how the heck did that happen? Ally MacLeod loses his smile as Hibernian score against Aberdeen.

What is Ally's secret? He has a simple philosophy. 'I just want to win,' he says. 'At everything. I even want to beat the kids at ludo.' What makes MacLeod tick, however, is his colossal drive, which incidentally did not go un-noticed outside football for, shortly before he left Ayr, he was asked to take on a £15 000-a-year job looking after the Scottish interests of a world-renowned firm.

He also had a successful sales career with Rio Tinto Zinc during his early years at Ayr when he was a part-time manager.

I have known Ally MacLeod since he started playing football and I will always remember him as one of the most entertaining wingers of all time – eccentric, of course, but a character, a card, and a player who attracted the fans.

He was brought up in Clydebank but, after his family home was bombed in the war, he moved to Glasgow's Mount Florida. While he was still at Queen's Park Secondary School he became a Third Lanark player, which was only fitting because the jolly old Thirds, gone alas now, were also a club of enthusiastic but often erratic talents, tinged to the end with that old-time idea that the game was the thing – something to be enjoyed.

Any idea MacLeod had that football was just a sport soon was driven out of his mind when, after a short spell with St Mirren, he joined Blackburn Rovers. There he learned to become a dedicated professional, obsessed in the English League way with the idea of winning. With Rovers, Ally played in the side which were runners-up in the First Division and beaten finalists in the FA Cup in 1960. When he returned to Scotland he captained Hibernian for a couple of seasons before moving on to Ayr United, first as player-coach, then manager.

There he learned his first lessons in publicity. He did so much to put the team and the town on the map that he was elected 'Citizen of the Year' in 1973.

His energy is tremendous. So is his pride and faith in his teams. Once when he felt Ayr were unlucky to lose to Celtic, he remarked to me after the game: 'Want to know the real score? It was Ayr United 1, Referee 3.' That's Ally.

His ebullience may become wearing and he is a non-stop talker. But he is never nasty, never bitter. Of course, he shouts at matches. But he is not abrasive. He likes people – and

people like him. He does not invite acrimony.

While some people see in him a tartan edition of Brian Clough, he could never make the enemies the outspoken Clough invited. As MacLeod says: 'Brian took every other team apart and told their managers how to run them. I don't do that. I concentrate only on my own team.

'Perhaps some managers would like to see me fall flat on my face but that's only human nature and I know I talk and make forecasts. That's me, though, and even if I am the most booed manager at away grounds I never mind.

'A manager has to drive or cajole. It doesn't matter really how you do it as long as you can motivate. I have a splendid coach in George Murray who looks after the details. I consider it's my job to get on with the wider scene.'

MacLeod is certainly not a mountebank. Neither does he court popularity by being weak or trying to placate his players. Every good manager needs a hard streak – and Ally has it. He has fined players for being out of line or late. He makes his staff go all out in exhausting cross-country runs. At the weekly trial match at Pittodrie, the losers, whether first team or reserves, have to report back in the afternoon for extra training.

But the MacLeod magic is working. He doubled the home gates inside a month. For instance, at the Pittodrie game with Motherwell in September the crowd was only 5500. In January when Motherwell returned to Aberdeen the gate was 16 177, which was an old-time attendance in the north.

Enthusiasm returned and programmes, developments tickets and souvenirs hit a new high.

Ally MacLeod genuinely likes people and has a capacity for self-help which is almost Victorian. And part of the reason for the increase in Aberdeen support has been the manager's willingness to meet and mix with the fans. He spends much of his leisure time

Oh dear, imagine them doing that after all I've told them. . . . Ally isn't happy with his boys at this stage. But you can't keep exuberant Mr MacLeod down for long. He's the eternal optimist – and the toast of Aberdeen.

with the supporters clubs and he leapt at the chance of doing an advertising stunt in the town, mainly because it meant he could meet the supporters.

He received £50 for the job and at once donated it to the players' kitty for their end-of-the-season night out.

What sums up MacLeod best are his thoughts when he looked back on his start at Pittodrie late in 1975. 'I believed I was going north on a rescue job. I thought I'd just watch the side for a month and then go to town and make changes. But I saw Aberdeen at Motherwell before I took over and they were murder.

'So I said to myself – What the hell, it's not my nature to go slow. I'll just change it now. I did it in three days and it has been working since then. And how the players have worked for me.'

Look out for cheerful Ally MacLeod going on to even greater things at Pittodrie . . . even though the team struggled at the end of the season and it proved that talk and personality alone can't win top success.

NOW THEN WHAT'S IT ALL ABOUT?

Football's a kaleidoscope of life and besides the joy of goals, the tragedy of mistakes and the ecstasy of victory, there is the head-scratching of mystery.

Football has its share of curious events and last season was no exception.

Suppose a visitor from Mars had suddenly arrived in Scotland and been taken to see matches, what would he have made of the incidents pictured here?

Do you know what it's all about?

Hell, they say, hath no fury like a footballer who believes he has been the victim of rank injustice. And that's what this vivid picture is all about. St Johnstone players protest bitterly and violently as referee Charlie Hutton decides a penalty by Alex Miller of Rangers and brilliantly saved by goalkeeper Derek Robertson of St Johnstone must be taken again. The ref stands firm. The kick is retaken. And this time Miller scores. For Saints it is an Ibrox tragedy.

Aw, come on, ref, it was never a penalty.
So says an angry Bobby Watson of
Motherwell in a game against Rangers at
Fir Park. But – that's where you're wrong,
Bobby, answers referee John Gordon. And a
penalty it was.

Fog and a crowd invasion brought a Celtic–
Hibernian match at Parkhead to a stop last
season. In the end, the Premier League game
was abandoned towards full time because
of the weather. Hibs weren't too happy.
They were leading 2–0. And the replayed
game was drawn.

That break-in had repercussions. Celtic
decided it was time to do something. The
result? The fence at Parkhead that keeps the
fans where they should be – on the terracing.

Well may you ask what this is all about.
For this is a most unusual occurrence. It's a
miskick by Celtic's Danny McGrain in a
match with Dundee. And a miskick by the
brilliant McGrain, one of the world's finest
backs, is as unusual as a cheer for a Celtic
goal at Ibrox by the Rangers fans.

A real puzzle here. It's a goal for Rangers against Hearts at Tynecastle. But — who scored it? Derek Johnstone, of Rangers? No indeed. It was a tragedy for Hearts centre-half Alan Anderson who headed the ball past his own keeper, Jim Cruickshank.

Fair's fair, though. Rangers also had their share of bad luck. And Tom Forsyth looks miserable as he does an Anderson — and deflects the ball past his goalie for the equalizer.

The only man who knows what's going on here is the referee. Celtic were convinced they had scored against Rangers. Colin Jackson of Rangers was certain they hadn't. Colin was correct. Offside was the decision.

This is what victory is about, an epic victory, that is. Motherwell have just come back after being two down to Celtic in the Scottish Cup-tie at Fir Park, to win 3–2 and manager Willie McLean shows his joy as he congratulates his players.

No, this isn't a match incident. It shows just how exhausting training can be. Especially the training of Rangers. Last season, manager Jock Wallace introduced a Superstar athletic contest – and this is how the lads felt after the completion of the 660-yard race final.

GREAT SCOTS-Meet an Entrancing Trio

Will Tommy be our World Cup Captain?

Anglos have not been the most popular players with the legions who watch internationals at Hampden. Even stars of the magnitude of Denis Law and Billy Bremner had their critics. And there are still groans from veterans who recall utter disasters, unknowns from south of the border who made surprise appearances in Scotland teams, disappointed and vanished from the international scene for all time.

Tommy Craig, however, is different. The little red-haired Newcastle United man appeals greatly to Scottish fans. For one thing, he is a master craftsman – and that's the type of player we love in Scotland. Skill is all to Tommy. He's also a natural captain and he earned high praise for the way he shepherded Scotland's Under-23 team in Europe last season.

It can't be long until Craig takes over the mantle of Billy Bremner and becomes captain of Scotland for a long, long time.

It would do no harm to try to build our World Cup team round one of the most sensible and inspiring players in football. Not only is he a splendid captain, he has the rare quality of making good players look great and ordinary players look good.

Craig always tries to set an example. He says: 'I am always deeply conscious of the kids watching me and because of that I try to do what's right.'

Tommy's one and only ambition was to become a footballer and he was so keen on the game that when he was about to leave Primary School and had the choice of three Secondary schools – he chose the one which had the best football team.

Although Tommy as a boy was a Celtic fan, he jumped at the chance of joining Aberdeen when he was fifteen. Three years later he became the youngest player to be transferred for £100 000 to Sheffield Wednesday.

Now he has moved on to Newcastle United and football life for the little Glasgow man has never looked better. But Tommy knows that football is not a bed of roses and he gives this advice to youngsters who are eager to follow in his footsteps:

'One thing you must learn in football is that it is futile to lose your temper. Not only do you penalize yourself, you penalize your club.

'Mind you, the one part of soccer life I hate is the time just before a match. Oh, those two or three hours before a game – how time drags!'

Tommy Craig has achieved practically all his ambitions in football. But there's one thing he still dreams of doing – leading Scotland to World Cup glory.

No player is more determined than Tommy Craig – so who's to say this dream won't come true as well. Every Scot is right behind Tommy in this one.

He's one of the Old Guard

The one position in football in which players seem to get better as they grow older is goal. And who realizes this more than Jim Cruickshank of Hearts? For Jim was recalled to international duty by Scotland manager Willie Ormond – at the age of 34.

The veteran Tynecastle keeper gives much of the credit for his comeback to manager John Hagart. 'John and I have a great relationship,' he said. 'I even enjoyed playing in the reserves for him, though I had been pretty browned off before and felt like

Tommy Craig, who could be Scotland's next World Cup captain.

packing it all in because I couldn't get a game in the first eleven.

'But when John took over it was different. Whenever I would moan about my lot he would say: "Forget about yourself. Look at the young fellows around you and think how your experience can help them."

'Sure enough I ended up helping the kids, giving them advice here and there and I really enjoyed that. That helped me, too, because when I was happy I was playing well. And then I was re-instated in the first team and was called up again for Scotland. I couldn't have been happier.'

What's the secret of the success of the man who could well emulate Celtic's Ronnie Simpson and play until he's grey? Certainly it's not fierce training. Grins Cruiky:

'I'm not the world's best trainer. I've never seen the point of doing all that running outfield players do. I can either do the same training as them or I can play in goal – but I can't do both.

'If I'm forced to do a lot of running I find that my legs go, all the spring goes out of them and I play like a clown.'

Perhaps Jim's secret is that he is a pressure player. 'I love the big-time atmosphere,' he says, 'and there's plenty of pressure nowadays in the Premier League.'

Cruickshank has been with Hearts for 16 years and he is playing better than at any other stage of his career. He puts it down to experience and makes the point that goalkeepers generally take longer to reach their peaks than players in other positions.

He adds: 'It wasn't until I was 28 or so that I really started playing. As you get older you learn to read the game better and can help other defenders by shouting instructions to them on the field, sort of manipulating them.'

If Jim has had his successes, he has also had his share of nightmares and he recalls a game not so many seasons ago against Arbroath when everyone thought he had chucked away three goals.

'It was the sun to blame,' said Cruiky. 'It was unbelievable. I had a cap on and my hands up to my eyes but the glare was terrible. I just couldn't see a thing and the balls flew past me into the net.

'It was a real blinder – but not the type of blinder I like to play.'

Jim's great games, however, more than make up for the few sad matches he's had.

Motherwell's Bobby-dazzler

Motherwell's Bobby Graham is another player beloved of the Scottish fans. Cute. Alert. Entrancing. Right out of the old school of master inside forwards – and more.

Bobby is also a quick-thinking attacker, who blends the old with the new and is the cool, calm ball player, purveyor and prince of magic moves every manager dreams of . . .

He is the perfect partner for Willie Pettigrew, ace striker – and no one knows that

Still going strong is Jim Cruickshank, the Hearts goalkeeper.

One of the best signings Motherwell ever made – Bobby Graham. Here he is with manager Ian St John, now with Portsmouth.

better than Willie, who says: 'Bobby is wonderful and he has done so much for me.'

Bobby is 31 but I don't think he's too old to play for Scotland and a cap for Graham would be some recognition for the part he has played in the success of Pettigrew. While Pettigrew has an undoubted scoring talent, he thrives on Graham's passes.

Says Bobby: 'I know the way Willie likes the ball. He prefers it played right through to him on his right so that he can run at the opposition. He's got to take it sometimes on his left, of course, but he's never so comfortable.'

Graham knows how strikers like to be fed. None better. He's had plenty of experience with the experts. He has always been able to read the way others play. At Liverpool he was alongside Roger Hunt, Alun Evans and Ian St John and they all liked the ball played to them differently. Bobby gave them perfect service.

Few players read the game better than the former Liverpool and Coventry forward.

THE CHANGING FACE OF FOOTBALL

Did the goalkeeper move before the penalty kick was taken? That has always been the cause of angry discussion on the terracings, especially in recent years when more and more keepers seem to be taking a chance and moving before the kick is taken.

Many people think it is unfair that goalies must stay rooted to the spot until the ball is actually kicked.

But there is good reason for the rule. A penalty provides the nearest approach to a gift goal, yet for years no restriction was placed on the movements of the keeper.

Two Scottish goalkeepers were the real reason for the law being altered in 1929. One was Rab McFarlane, of Morton, whose ploy was to snatch off his cap and dance like a dervish to put the penalty kick taker off his shot. The other was Tom Farquharson, of Cardiff City, who used to stand at the

back of the net and, as the kicker ran up to the ball, darted forward with outspread arms.

Both keepers saved so many penalties because of those bizarre actions that the penalty kick rule had to be changed.

The game as we know it at present owes a lot to our own pioneers, Queen's Park, who introduced new rules which have stood football in good stead.

But one by-law Queen's put into the books in 1876 isn't observed to any great degree today: 'That no player shall, under any pretence whatever, use improper language on the field.'

Others were more important and these included: To use a goal bar instead of a tape . . . To adopt a fixed half-time instead of switching ends after every goal . . . To throw the ball in with two hands and not one.

It is fascinating to consider how the rules of football have changed since the game began in the middle of the last century.

Many have been changed because individual players, like the two goalkeepers, exposed weaknesses that few folk realized existed.

One of the most important was the offside law. In the old days, a player was offside if there were not three or more opponents between himself and the opponents' goal. Enter, then, Willie McCracken, the famous

Football's changed, so they say. Or has it? How about these pictures, one taken in 1901, the other in 1976?

This was the triumphant Rangers team which won the League championship and Glasgow Cup in season 1900–01. This team collected a total of 174 Scottish caps among them.

Here's a star of today, Stewart Kennedy, Rangers goalkeeper. But look at that cap! In contrast to the rest of Stewart's mod gear, the bonnet looks as though it could have been worn by one of the 1900 heroes.

Newcastle United back. Instead of staying near his own goal, he operated near the half-way line. As opposing forwards moved down-field, he walked a few yards, leaving rivals offside.

Into such a fine art did Willie develop this plot that he often left all five opposing forwards offside.

What a bind, though, for the fans this was. Constant stoppages for free kicks ruined Newcastle's fixtures. And when less skilful players began the offside game there appeared to be more whistling than football in the 90 minutes.

In 1925 the rule was altered so that a player was not offside so long as there were two players between himself and the goal. Three were no longer needed.

But that change had far-reaching effects. Dribbling became a lost art. Speedy wingers and dead-shot centre-forwards, working in partnership, scored greater numbers of goals than ever before. Then came another counter-measure, the stopper centre-half.

Talking about whistling . . . did you know that it wasn't until 1878 that a referee blew a blast for the first time – at Hampden Park. Until then the rules said that all the referee had to do was give a signal.

So referees controlled play by waving a flag or handkerchief when an infringement had been committed but, in the excitement of the game, these wavings were apt to be ignored. The whistle was the answer to all the problems.

Nevertheless, there is no mention of a whistle in the rules so a referee who waves a flag can't be criticized.

The throw-in has been the subject of violent controversey and the rule has been changed several times. It was Sam Weaver, another Newcastle player, who was respon-

sible for one amendment. This strong wing-half could throw the ball from the touch-line right into the goal-mouth and the rules were altered to make the thrower keep both feet on the touch-line.

And it was a player who had the authorities deciding you can't kick the ball twice in succession at a corner. He was Sam Chedgzoy, the Everton right winger, the first man to make history because of a new law that said a goal could be scored direct from a corner.

The astute Sam dribbled the ball right into the goal area and put the ball into the net. Red-faced legislators had quickly to introduce a clause which said the kicker couldn't touch the ball more than once.

There have been several versions of the penalty kick law. Up until 1891 the distance of the area from goal was only 12 yards as against 18 yards today and the ball could be kicked from any point on the 12-yard line.

The first penalty as we know it today was scored in 1891 by Douglas Dick, who later became chairman of Kilmarnock, but who notched that historic goal from the spot when he was playing for Morton against Celtic.

Some of the early laws make you wonder how they ever played football. For instance, the first law in the old days said: 'The maximum length of ground shall be 200 yds and the maximum breadth 100 yds.' Certainly the players had plenty of running to do in those days for the law today states that the maximum length of the playing field will not be more than 130 yds.

It wasn't until 1893 that goal nets were introduced – and thus heated arguments about whether the ball had crossed the line stopped.

WHEN GLASGOW BELONGED TO EUROPE

Glasgow, dear old, grey Glasgow town, belonged to Europe on the night of 12 May 1976. It was fiesta time in Scotland, a night of glamorous football, a merry night of revelry, a night of drama and fun unparalleled in the city's history.

The night Glasgow became Europe's capital, with revelry going on into the wee sma' hours – aye, in the city that begins to die, albeit noisily, around 10 p.m. – was the occasion of the European Cup Final at Hampden between Bayern Munich and St Etienne. Glasgow decided to live it up for the big game, to make the Continental visitors feel at home. Pubs were allowed to stay open until 3 a.m. And the city had never seen such post-midnight merry-making, not even at Hogmanay.

A crowd of 54 864 were at Hampden whose wrinkled old face was gaily cosmetically disguised for the evening to see the big game. Alas, it took its predictable course, with Bayern beating the gallant Frenchmen by 1–0. The coolly assured professionals of West Germany won, just as most of us thought they would. And although the volatile St Etienne, who had earlier dismissed Rangers from the European Cup, played with flair they seemed to have little faith in their ability to pierce the flexible German defence.

So the game turned out to be something of a disappointment for the crowd who had done so much to make it a gala affair. It was really all too professional and there was mild booing at the end for the Germans, although they didn't deserve it. After all, they won because they were the team with the style and confidence, even if that style isn't what British fans relish, a style which calls for players to play well within themselves and give nothing away.

Bayern may not have been the most exciting team in the world but no one at Hampden on 12 May would have liked to pick opponents in Europe to beat them.

Their goal came at the right time. St Etienne were playing with a touch of old-fashioned precision, spreading the play neatly and concentrating on attack. Then the Germans scored in 58 minutes – a simple goal, but stylish – a goal which proved they are Europe's kings of smash and grab. Gerd Muller, hardly seen and beautifully marked out of the game by the towering Argentinian, Piazza, started it. For once he was fouled by his shadow, Piazza.

It looked just another innocuous free-kick – until the immaculate Franz Beckenbauer tapped the ball to Franz Roth.

Before the French defence realized what was happening, Roth had whipped the ball into the net.

We all knew there was no way St Etienne could come back. In a last-gasp effort to pull the game out of the fire they brought on injured winger Dom Rocheteau, the man who had done so much to rout Rangers.

The winger showed a few scintillating touches, but not sufficient to worry the so-capable Germans.

75

St Etienne were the team Scotland supported in the European Cup Final at Hampden. Here are some of the French players having a look at Hampden before the big game.

If the final never reached the heights of the never-to-be-forgotten Real Madrid–Eintracht match, also at Hampden, it had its moments, for the alleged experts, at least.

Bayern did just what they had to do, and no more. They are not flashy, they are not adventurous, they don't take chances, they'd never get an Iron Cross for audacious attacking. But they are utterly efficient. It was not the football Scots love. It was, nonetheless, the football that pays in this modern age. Patience is the keynote of the Munich game. And you have the impression that with superstars like Beckenbauer, Roth, Hoeness and Schwarzenbeck all they have to do in the unlikely event of disaster striking, is to raise their game as they can and equalize.

It's true St Etienne had bad luck several times, hitting woodwork. The Scots were right behind the French. But even their encouragement couldn't help the cause of the Auld Alliance, because St Etienne didn't have the professionalism of Bayern.

It wasn't the most distinguished final old Hampden has seen. But it was modern football, the kind of football that brings success in Europe, the kind of football which took three European Cups to Bayern in three seasons.

There was little art about Munich. Technique is what they concentrate on, cold science is what they base all their play on. Built by logic and computer, the Germans took the heart out of what should have been a magnificent final. There was little entertainment provided by the men from Munich.

But they have outstanding players. Like Inter Milan of the last decade, they could, one feels, play brilliant, entertaining football. They don't choose to. Why should they? They are the emperors of Europe.

No wonder one sighs for the football we once knew and loved, the football played by Real and the Hungarians. No wonder football becomes a yawn and no wonder the fans are deserting the game. The spice, the adventure has gone. So has the poetry and the drama. The soccer field is a chess-board.

Munich may well be the best team in the world. We Scots still don't fancy them, even though we know in our hearts we have no-one in our country with a chance of beating them. This is just not football to us.

At the end and long into the night, Scots and French were allies, drinking companions and great mates. They walked arm in arm still waving their fluttering flags of green and white, despite their dejection over the result and demanded wine instead of haufs and hauf pints in the bustling pubs.

The victorious Bavarians were nowhere to be seen for they had fallen into every cliché about well-organized Germanic. thoroughness by retreating to their package-tour suburban hotels for their well-organized celebrations with the hock and beer they had brought over.

But the Glasgow streets were a sea-green tide of St Etienne supporters and their Scottish friends and Glasgow warmed to the French with an enthusiasm which overwhelmed the visitors.

It had been Glasgow's most hectic 24 hours in years, with shops and pubs and hotels calling it a 'multi-million pound bonanza'.

The one mystery about the game was: what happened to the 30 000 missing fans? There was a capacity of 85 000 but only 54 864 turned up. The explanation was that when a game is televised live many fans don't turn up even though they buy tickets. Nearly 80 000 tickets had been sold.

It was the most expensive match ever staged in Scotland, with the cheapest ticket costing £1.50 and the top stand seat £8.

Earlier, Bayern had criticized Hampden as the venue because they didn't fancy the pitch and felt there wouldn't be a big enough crowd but withdrew their protests and skipper Beckenbauer said: 'Hampden was perfect for us. We have no complaints.'

Certainly Glasgow had no complaints about their night of revelry.

The teams were:

Bayern: Maier, Hansen, Horsemann, Schwarzenbeck, Beckenbauer, Roth, Rummenigge, Durnberger, Muller, Hoeness, Keppellmann.

St. Etienne: Curkovic, Janvion, Repellini, Piazza, Lopez, Batheney, P. Revelli, Larque, H. Revelli, Santini, Sarramanga. Sub: Rocheteau.

Referee: K. Palotai, Hungary.

THE FLOWERS O'SCOTLAND

Hampden exploded with the greatest roar of exultation, excitement – and laughter – the famous old ground had ever known.

It was the afternoon of 15 May 1976 – the afternoon in which dreams came true for the Scots in the crowd of 85,165. Harsh nationalism was in the damp atmosphere before the annual battle between Scotland and England, shown in the ecstatic singing of the new 'anthem' which is called 'Oh, Flower O' Scotland', the insults to the few Sassenachs on the terracings, which were a sea of yellow Lions Rampant, and the frantic encouragement of the Scottish team even before they appeared on the pitch. It was heavy aggression, typical of the fixture and the electricity in the air couldn't be affected by the pre-match rain.

Scotland were packed with confidence, which wasn't to be wondered at for manager Willie Ormond had turned his team into hot-shots again. With the cool Don Masson, of Queens Park Rangers – and at the age of 29 – in the team to bring old-style passing power and introduce the velvet touch which used to be the pride of Scottish soccer, the new-look side had done well in the home internationals, beating Wales 3–1 and Ireland 3–0 at Hampden.

Now it was the crunch, the big game – let's face it – the game every Scot wants to win even more than the World Cup: the international against England, an England who were struggling.

Scottish fans could hardly wait for the kick-off, and what a reception they gave their heroes, kitted out dandily in a modern strip, as they ran onto the field! This was the line-up:

Scotland: Rough (Partick Thistle), McGrain (Celtic), Donachie (Manchester City), Forsyth (Rangers), Jackson (Rangers), Rioch (Derby County), Dalglish (Celtic), Masson (Queens Park Rangers), Jordan (Leeds United), Gemmill (Derby County – captain), Gray (Leeds United).

England: Clemence (Liverpool), Todd (Derby County), Mills (Ipswich Town), Thompson (Liverpool), McFarland (Derby County), Kennedy (Liverpool), Keegan (Liverpool), Channon (Southampton), Pearson (Manchester United), Francis (Queens Park Rangers – captain), Taylor (Crystal Palace).

Referee: Karoly Palotai, Hungary.

The downpour had made the pitch slippery and the chanting and cheering for Scotland quickly turned into a gasp of horror as disaster almost hit in the first minute. From a free kick, the ball was allowed to pass through to Alan Rough and Scottish hearts stood still as it bounced awkwardly and skidded past the keeper's hands. Luckily, the ball struck Rough on the face

The goal which had all Scotland singing. Kenny Dalglish beats goalkeeper Ray Clemence with this shot at Hampden in the international against England.

And here's poor Ray Clemence who committed the worst goalkeeping blunder of all by allowing Dalglish's shot to slip between his legs.

and was cleared. But that freak bounce made the players apprehensive about the turf and there was an unreal slowness about the game.

Although England played an unnatural game for them – trying to slow play in the Continental manner – Scotland were first to settle and there was a thrill when a fine header by Dalglish looked net-bound, until Ray Clemence, with instinctive acrobatics, saved.

But in the 11th minute there was horror for Scotland. England centre-half Roy McFarland broke through after intercepting a bad Scottish pass. He went on and sent over a fine cross which found Channon who, with spectacular power, headed the ball past a transfixed Rough.

Credit Scotland with skill and courage. There was furious reaction to that dent to their pride, the niceties of pace were forgotten and the game exploded. Blue shirts swamped the England penalty area. Thompson was harrassed into slicing the ball over his own bar. Jordan headed narrowly over. Aggression was unbridled. And it brought the goal Scotland deserved.

In 18 minutes joy returned to Hampden. Scotland equalized with a simple yet bril-

Below: Don Masson scores Scotland's first goal at Hampden.

Opposite: One of Scotland's heroes against England was Joe Jordan, as good in defence as in attack as you can see from this picture, in which the striker is clearing in his own penalty area.

Overleaf: Scotland centre-half Colin Jackson looks on as England's Kevin Keegan tries a shot.

liantly taken goal. When a corner from Eddie Gray came belting over, not an English defender moved a muscle to clear it. But Don Masson did. He nodded his head superbly, the ball flew into the net and pandemonium reigned all over Hampden.

Soon the Scottish attack were taking inspiration from the skills of Danny McGrain, surely the best back in Europe. He was brilliant in attack and defence and, in front of him, Dalglish and the precise Masson played football that pierced the heart of the English defence.

It was as well for England that Roy McFarland, just back in the side after injury, was in splendid form for he was the one man who stood between the brave and skilful charging of Joe Jordan and the waves of hectic Scottish attacks.

Scotland had taken command and England weren't allowed to settle to any kind of orderly game.

Indeed, Scotland should have finished ahead at half-time. The fact they didn't made referee Palotai the most unpopular man in Scotland since Butcher Cumberland.

Half-time was nearing as Ken Dalglish set off on one of the most fascinating runs Hampden has seen. On and on he went. The English defence was outwitted. Out came Clemence. Dalglish swerved. But the goal-keeper dived at him and brought him down. A penalty? Only one man didn't think so. The referee. He shook his head, pointed for a goal-kick and then whistled for half-time.

The booing almost brought down the Hampden stand. And the referee's statement afterwards didn't help him much. He said: 'I blew for half-time before Clemence made his tackle. Otherwise it would have been a penalty.' Nevertheless, the Hampden thousands, and millions on TV, clearly saw the referee point for a goal-kick after the incident. So it couldn't have been the interval.

Scotland looked bitterly angry when the second half began. Soon they were in full cry.

And then came the moment of delight, the moment that brought the loudest Hampden roar. Jordan ran magnificently on the left. Dalglish brought his cross under control. Alas, he only half hit his shot. But that attempt in the 49th minute will never be forgotten by the Scots who saw it – or by poor Ray Clemence in the England goal.

It was a moment of gloating delight for the Scottish crowd – that moment of supreme irony that pushed the international their way. The tartan-tammied men who had suffered so cruelly over the years from the nervous paralysis that so often affects their goalkeepers against England now saw Clemence, one of the few world-class keepers, surrender a goal with the kind of error that would bring embarrassment in a game on Glasgow Green.

The keeper – whose work is generally as close to being flawless as any player in the world – appeared perfectly positioned to take the Dalglish shot, especially as it was slackly delivered.

Then, to the amazement and ecstasy of the Scots, Clemence boobed as badly as any Scottish keeper at Wembley.

He allowed the ball to pass between his legs and into the net. Scotland had gone ahead. Jubilation floated with bagpipes' strains of triumph up to the grey clouds. As an Englishman said sadly of Clemence: 'No-one since Churchill had seemed less likely to let his country down.'

That was the end. The invaders knew in their hearts they could never come back. Scotland were serenely in command. And the crowd saw Alan Rough dribble round Kevin Keegan well outside the penalty box before sending on a pass to Danny McGrain.

It was a matter of playing out time. England brought on two substitutes, Cherry and Doyle, but it made no difference. Scotland took off the obviously unfit Eddie Gray and replaced him with Derek Johnstone.

Scotland were content to play the ball around while McGrain and Dalglish now and again pranced into action which worried England sick.

Yet the game ended with a huge sigh of relief. Almost on the whistle Channon broke through and an undeserved draw seemed certain for England – until Tom Forsyth, over whom so much controversy had centred before the game but who had played a hero's part for his country, came to the rescue with one of the best-timed tackles

Hampden has ever seen and robbed the English striker in the nick of time.

So Scotland took revenge, cruel, memorable and complete, for the massacre of Wembley the previous season, and that gleaming silver British Championship trophy was proudly paraded by the Scots in a lap of honour.

Scotland had clearly been the better team in a match which was more exciting than inspired, even though the midfield players did not approach the fluent mastery of their performances against the less demanding opposition of Wales and Ireland. The pleasure of the 2–1 victory was substantially in-

This is the man who makes the new Scotland tick – Don Masson, of Queen's Park Rangers, having a word with Pat Jennings of Ireland after an international at Hampden.

creased by the awareness that if the match could be said to have had two real stars they were both wearing blue – McGrain at full-back and Forsyth at sweeper. But there wasn't a failure in the Scotland team.

Scotland, her players rampant and her supporters riotous, were once again undisputed masters of British football, after a day which had started with nervous misgivings and ended with deep pleasure. For it was a win carved from pure professionalism over England, who were supposed to have a copyright on the basic nuts and bolts of the game. And the future looks brighter now that there is a competent, serious and studied pattern to Scotland.

Scottish football has so often been about instant glory or great disillusionment, that the thread of continuous improvement is gloriously welcome.

Scotland ended the season unbeaten, with two wins over Denmark, a draw against Rumania and victories over Switzerland, Wales, Northern Ireland and England. The team which took us to the World Cup has been replaced with another, even better. Only twice have Scotland lost since they left West Germany and the World Cup unbeaten.

And it's good to realize that Ormond's lads appear to have mastered the art of winning without deserting our native concept that football is meant to be played going forward.

The only regret is that Fred Martin, Frank Haffey and Stewart Kennedy weren't there to see the ball go through Clemence's legs. Cruel? Perhaps. But how often have Scotland suffered with goalkeeping nerves?

It was the first time Scotland had won the home championship outright since 1967, the triple crown for the first time in 13 years.

There must be applause for manager Ormond – so often criticized was Willie who chose the pattern for the team and found the players to fit it.

Probably the most important aspect of the win was that Scotland continued to play smoothly, crisply and intelligently. There was a new discipline in the team who hit back after being a goal down but still played controlled football.

Gone was the bitter animosity, the fearsome determination to outkick England which previous Scottish sides have shown.

This was a new composed Scotland – a Scotland which can at least go into the World Cup with a chance.

THE TEAM ALL THE GIANTS FEAR,
by Harry Johnston, Montrose FC

By Harry Johnston, Montrose midfield player

Montrose provided Scottish football with some of its biggest surprises last season – but the fact that we did so well came as no shock to myself or my team-mates at Links Park.

For while a lot of clubs, both bigger and smaller than ourselves, have put the emphasis on strength and courage in recent seasons, the attitude at Montrose has never altered since I joined them five years ago.

Both managers I have served under at the club, Alex Stuart and Kenny Cameron, base their ideas on just one thing – SKILL.

While other clubs have forgotten that very important ingredient, Montrose have worked towards playing attractive skilful football at all times – and look how well it worked last season.

Back in August 1975, before the start of the new League set-up, most people had us down as one of the clubs least likely to succeed in the First Division. They reckoned we would be mighty lucky to escape relegation.

Within a couple of months these same people had eaten a whole lot of words and, with just a few breaks at the right time, many of them would have had indigestion before the end of the season!

Right from the start we made good progress in the League Cup and the League. All through the League programme we were never out of the leading bunch and we won

our way to the quarter-finals of the League Cup by finishing on top of a section that contained East Fife, St. Mirren and Raith Rovers.

And it was in that League Cup quarter-final that our skill brought us one of the biggest upsets of the League Cup – in any year.

Paired with Hibs, one of the favourites to win the trophy, we almost held out for what would have been a great goal-less draw at Easter Road. But they scored near the end for a 1–0 win.

We still fancied our chances but, within a couple of minutes of the start of the return game on a wet and windy night at Links Park we went further behind when Arthur Duncan scored.

It stayed that way until half-time . . . but the next 75 dramatic minutes will be remembered as long as football is played in the town.

Bobby Livingstone, a player who is unstoppable when he hits his best form, got back the first goal and then Leslie Barr, our dead-ball expert, sent our supporters wild with excitement by scoring a second, making it 2–2 on aggregate at the end of 90 minutes.

Of course, the people who had doubted our ability at the start of the season now started to question our staying power, reckoning that 30 minutes' extra-time against a full-time team would see us off after threatening to cause a bit of an upset.

In fact, it was the Easter Road side and

Harry Johnston, Montrose

who saw the game will ever try to suggest that the Ibrox side were four goals better than us on the night.

In fact, at half-time in that game, there were a few signs of concern in the Rangers dressing room and on the Hampden terracings among the faithful Light Blue following. Leslie Barr had given us the lead just before half-time from the penalty spot.

And even when Rangers did get going, we missed a couple of great chances that could have made the score much more respectable.

It was definitely these two League Cup performances against Rangers and Hibs that saw all of Scottish football suddenly sit up and take notice of the good things that were happening at Links Park. They also cost us our manager, Alex Stuart.

Alex had, of course, been doing a great job at the club for over five years but, not long after the League Cup run, he moved to the Premier League with Ayr United.

Within days, the board had named Kenny Cameron, our former centre-forward, as the new manager. And, surely, there never has been a smoother managerial take-over in Scottish soccer.

Kenny's ideas on the game are similiar to Alex's, and the players were happy just to go on playing for the club.

We went on to finish third in the table behind Partick Thistle and Kilmarnock – about 10 places higher than our 'friends' had predicted – and then we followed that up by scaring the life out of Hearts in the Scottish Cup.

After beating Morton and Raith Rovers, we were paired with the Tynecastle team in the quarter-finals at Links Park. How close we came to giving them the kind of beating we had handed out to their Edinburgh neighbours a few months earlier.

After a goal-less first half, Malcolm Lowe gave us the lead early in the second before our skipper, Dave McNicoll, headed through his own goal. That sort of equalizer might have upset a lot of teams, but not us.

their supporters who were upset at the finish of a tension-packed night.

For in extra-time Les Barr scored an incredible goal, hitting a clearance from inside his own half of the field that somehow deceived goalkeeper Jim McArthur in the back of the net.

That amazing goal gave us a 3–1 win on the night, a 3–2 victory on aggregate, and a place in the semi-finals against Rangers at Hampden.

All right, I know that Rangers beat us 5–1 in that game but I don't think anyone

Soon we were ahead again, through Ian Stewart.

It seemed we were through to our first ever Scottish Cup semi-final but, in injury time, Graham Shaw made it 2–2.

This was a heart-breaking way to be held in a cup-tie but it didn't affect our belief that we could still do it in the replay. When I scored early in the game at Tyncastle things looked good for us and even more so when Leslie Barr netted from a penalty two minutes later to make it 2–0.

I'll say this for Hearts. They don't know when they are beaten. They came cracking back at us with goals from Shaw, again, and Willie Gibson. And, at the end of extra-time, it was again 2–2.

The third game was at Muirton Park, Perth, and once again we were first to score, through Jimmy Cant. We had another goal disallowed early in the second-half and eventually Shaw scored his third goal of the tie to make it 1–1.

Extra-time would not have been necessary that night if Dave McNicholl hadn't seen his shot in the very last minute of the 90 hit the post and come back into play.

It's on record now, of course, that Ralph Callachan scored for Hearts in extra-time to take them into the semi-finals. But, after we had recovered from our initial disappointment, we knew that we had once again proved the point I made at the start – that skill is really important at Montrose.

Naturally, there are other things that go to make us a great little club. After that 2–2 draw with Hearts at Tynecastle, for instance, our chairman, Willie Johnston, announced on the bus trip back home that the committee had decided to pay us players the bonus that had been agreed upon had we won.

Money isn't everything but, when you consider the number of disputes in the game over bonus money which has been promised but not paid, it does make a change to hear about a bonus being paid when the result wasn't achieved. For me, that is just one of the reasons why Montrose will continue to be one of the happy, attractive things about Scottish football.

IS SOCCER TOO TOUGH?

Scottish football is becoming too tough. That's the view of St Mirren manager Alex Ferguson – and he expressed it forcibly last season.

That's more than a little interesting. Because Alex, an outstanding player not so long ago, was hardly one of the meekest stars in the game.

Said Alex: 'I'm inclined to believe Scottish football is in danger of sliding into the state the English game was in five years ago.' And after a match in which his team were involved with deadly rivals, Partick Thistle, he snapped: 'Football died the death out there.'

Manager Ferguson feels there's too much tackling from behind, too much going over the ball, so that the skilful players don't have a chance.

'This,' he added, 'is what happened in England five years ago. But now tackling from behind is illegal in the south and players of the calibre of Kevin Keegan of Liverpool and the lively Manchester United players of Tommy Docherty are getting a chance to play real football again.'

Is Alex Ferguson right? Is Scottish soccer too rough?

Certainly the Premier League revealed a hardening in attitude. But our football is still tame compared to that of England even now – and I realize the game south of the border has been cleaned up recently.

On the other hand, just have a look at these photographs – and then go on arguing about whether Alex Ferguson is right or wrong. . . .

90

It's agony for Danny McGrain of Celtic as he is brought down in a game against Motherwell.

Opposite: This time the man feeling the pain is Motherwell's Gregor Stevens as he is brought down by a tackle from — Danny McGrain!

Below: Aye, it's gey tough game, says Dundee back Bobby Wilson, who had a headache for days following a knock in a hard match.

Overleaf: Tackles are always fierce when Rangers and Aberdeen clash as you can see from this incident involving Martin Henderson and Derek Johnstone facing a tough Dons' challenge.

Aberdeen are also unlikely to draw back when they meet the might of Celtic, and Miller and Hair just get in in time to stop Kenny Dalglish, who goes full length in his bid for a goal.

Motherwell's Willie Pettigrew is always a danger to defences – so Eddie Thomson of Aberdeen makes sure the lively leader doesn t get past on this occasion.

Is Peter Marinello of Motherwell saying 'Take that' to Celtic's Steve Murray? No, Peter tries to get in a shot.

A desperate raid by Bobby McKean of Rangers is foiled by Alan Anderson of Hearts and his defensive partner, Roy Kay, who takes a nasty tumble.

All the determination needed in modern football is shown in the expressions of Hearts' Jefferies and Busby and Dumbarton's Muir as they go for the ball.

Former Scotland captain Billy Bremner stands on no ceremony as he stops a Queen's Park Rangers player getting in a tackle against his Leeds United colleague, Peter Lorimer, also a Scottish international.

Meet the battling MacDonalds. Roddy, of Celtic, and Ian, of St Johnstone, engage in a teethy struggle.

So – you think Scottish soccer is too tough? You feel, like Alex Ferguson, that they're not as torrid in action, not as determined to win at all costs down in England?

Well, just look at this picture – it's from England last season . . . and you may change your mind. . . .

I feel the real truth is that football is still a tough game, whether it's played in Scotland or Switzerland, and long may it remain that way.

Football's a game for men – and often tempers are bound to snap, tackles become too wild. But in the end it's a game of skill and healthy rivalry, even at the top level.

WHAT'S THE TRUTH ABOUT ENGLISH FOOTBALL? Two Scottish Stars have Different Views

Iain Phillip, of Dundee, and Alex Reid, of Dundee United, rivals in tense Tayside derby games last season, have one thing in common. They returned to their respective clubs after spells in England. Here they discuss their views of English football and their careers in general.

By Dundee defender Iain Phillip

I had almost exactly a year with Crystal Palace in the English First and Second Divisions – and it took me twice as long to recover from the experience.

Iain Phillip, Dundee

What should have been a dream come true, a £100 000-plus transfer from a Scottish provincial club to a top one in the Big Smoke certainly didn't work out that way.

But let me make it clear that I am not knocking English football out of sight. It just didn't work out in my case, that's all.

The real trouble was that soon after I arrived at Selhurst Park I realized that Palace felt they had lashed out a great deal of money on a midfield player – and that is something I never was and never will be.

I had played in midfield with Dundee but I knew firmly in my own mind that my best position was in the middle of the defence.

But Palace, struggling near the foot of the First Division at that time, insisted that I play in the role they wanted from me.

Let me say that it isn't all that difficult to play in midfield down there — up to a point. Opponents are quite happy to give you yards of space in midfield and you can look good by simply hitting long balls all over the place.

But, in order to be really effective in that position south of the border, a player has to make an impact in and around his opponents' penalty area, too.

That's where I really found it a terrible struggle. It was something completely foreign to me. I suffered and so did the club.

Malcolm Allison arrived at Selhurst Park but could not prevent us from slipping into the Second Division despite spending a lot of money on other players.

Maybe some of my difficulties did result from that big price tag and not being able to justify it, though I prefer to believe it was mainly due to playing out of position.

In fact, even playing at the back on a couple of occasions, I found it difficult to find my form. I was having a thoroughly miserable time of it.

And very soon I discovered just how difficult it was to play football to the best of your ability when confidence has been eaten away.

With Palace and myself continuing to struggle in Division Two, I eventually got the chance to return to Dundee, for about half the cost.

I didn't exactly jump at the chance. After all, it was a bit like the Prodigal Son returning after making a mess of things with his big chance. Eventually, after talking things over with my wife and thinking the whole thing out, I did decide to move back to Tayside.

Any thought of picking up where I had left off quickly vanished, however. I soon began to realize just how much my confidence had been affected by my year in the south.

Even when Dundee got to the League Cup Final and beat Celtic 1–0 in 1973 at Hampden, soon after I returned, I wasn't completely happy.

For two years, in fact, I struggled to settle down again, although I must admit that a series of niggling injuries didn't help.

I consider that it was only last season that my form started to return. Happily, that was at the start of a new era in Scottish football, with the arrival of the Premier League.

I know a lot of people have reservations about the new set-up but I think everyone agrees that more competition was necessary. Maybe it has gone just a little too far with just too much pressure on players and managers but it had to be tried.

Eventually, the Premier League or some other set-up will remove the necessity for top Scottish players to move south of the border to make their names and their money . . . and I'll be first to applaud.

By Dundee United midfield player Alex Reid

The new set-up in Scottish football last season meant a whole lot of extra pressure on everyone in the game, not least the managers. Hardly a week seemed to pass without someone in the hot-seat getting a blast from his bosses on the board or the fans.

But I'll certainly not forget the help and the opportunities given to me by the two managers under whom I played last season.

First there was Joe Gilroy, who took over at Morton early in the season after a spell in Icelandic football. He arrived at Cappielow when I was struggling to get into shape following a cartilage operation.

Joe spent a lot of extra time with me, personally supervising my fight back to complete fitness, during which time I lost almost a stone in weight.

Of course, there were times when the effort didn't seem worthwhile but Joe kept at me, telling me constantly that better things were around the corner if I stuck to my fitness programme.

But even he could not have known just how right he was about to be proved. Suddenly, at the turn of the year, I got the chance to join Dundee United, the club I had left four years earlier to sign for Newcastle United.

Those four years previously I had been

Alex Reid, Dundee United

desperate to leave Tannadice and try my luck in England. But when United gave me the chance to rejoin them I didn't have to be asked a second time.

Without being disrespectful to Morton and the First Division, the Premier League had already proved highly competitive. I was on my way back to Tayside in a flash.

So you can see that I will always be grateful to Joe Gilroy for whipping me back into shape and to Jim McLean at Dundee United for giving me a second chance with the club.

I say that even though United were involved in relegation trouble when I joined them and continued to toil. Perhaps the new League set-up put just too much pressure on everyone concerned but there are no complaints from me on that score.

I certainly found the Premier League a far greater test with United the second time around than I had done with them four years earlier. For me it was quite like playing in the English First Division – and I had loved that with Newcastle.

I really enjoyed my two years in Geordieland. The whole set-up appealed to me, particularly the big crowds and the atmosphere. Off the field, too, the set-up is so different, with just about every club having their own private training ground. That has to help.

Of course, it all comes back to money. I reckon we could catch up if we had the resources. Motherwell were really the only club that decided to splash out in a big way to stake a claim for success when the new set-up came along.

They bought a couple of players and really had a go at winning the top honours. And they didn't do a bad job, even though they failed to land among the trophies.

Perhaps one of these years, more of the clubs will be able to pour money into the game and have a go as Motherwell did.

Then, I am certain, we'll have football as good as in England . . . or anywhere else for that matter.

ONE HUNDRED YEARS OF SIZZLING THISTLE-Manager Bertie Auld reveals the Secrets of the Good Old Jags

Everyone likes Partick Thistle. They are a club who have always liked to play entertaining soccer. And they have probably provided more laughs than anyone else in football.

Even their greatest triumph, a Scottish Cup victory in the 1921 final, could have been achieved only by the rollicking men of Firhill – for it was a win which contained everything from near disaster to Charlie Chaplin comedy.

To reach the final they played four ties but because of replays it took them ten desperate games before they met Rangers in the final. Then there was a row about the cup final venue. Celtic Park was chosen but only 28 000 spectators turned up because the admission charge had been increased to two shillings.

Finally, Thistle were so badly hit by injury that Jimmy McMenemy, the former Celtic star who had become the Jags' coach, was forced to take the field in a playing role.

But Thistle won – because Rangers' Jimmy Bowie had to leave the pitch to don a new pair of pants, his own having been torn. And when he was off. John Blair scored the goal that won the Scottish Cup for Thistle.

'Huh, all very funny, I grant you,' says Partick Thistle manager Bertie Auld. 'But that's been Thistle's biggest trouble, getting rid of the comedy tag which has dogged us all down the years.'

And perhaps the most formidable task of the former Celtic star was to make the jolly old Jags forget that they were best known as the Unpredictables. 'I hated that description,' said the manager. 'It's all right for the reporters to write that Thistle invariably provided the unexpected – thrills and comedy, triumph followed by disaster. But you can't afford to be happy-go-lucky in modern football. And I felt it was my job to provide a new image for Partick Thistle.'

And that's what Bertie did last season – brilliantly. For Thistle became the Consistents in Scottish football and won the First Division title.

Like most astute managers who have contrived to stay in a job Bertie Auld is a graduate of the best football school of all – the college of hard knocks. Bertie is dapper, articulate, smooth – his appearance matching the play which made him one of the great Scottish inside-forwards. But he knows better than most that artistry alone cannot win honours in soccer today.

Bertie was with Celtic under Jock Stein and inevitably some of the magic of the game's greatest manager rubbed off. Explaining Thistle's success, Auld said:

'I've always believed in attacking teams. But now I realize when you're going forward you've got to make sure you've not left the back door open. I remember Thistle playing a Continental team in a friendly in my early days as a manager. We were winning 4–1 and I put on a couple of strikers. We ended up scraping home 4–3. I learned a lot from that but I still like to see my boys going forward when they can. That's what brings in the fans.'

Bertie Auld learned something of the business of management as a player watching the best in action. When he went south to Birmingham he was managed by Gil Merrick – 'A great guy', according to Bertie,

The man behind the Partick Thistle success – manager Bertie Auld, not so long ago a star forward with Celtic.

who also learned a lot from coach, Joe Mallett – 'the best at his game in England'. Then he came back to Scotland to listen to

the wise words of Stein. Adds Bertie: 'Don't forget I also had a spell under Eddie Turnbull with Hibernian – and there are few better managers or coaches in football than Eddie.'

The Firhill manager thinks the hardest thing for a manager to do is to get through to his lads what he's trying to do. 'Every player in the team must play for each other and not for himself,' he says. And Bertie recalls what happened at the start of the season . . .

'We won three games because the boys played as a team. They worked really hard and they worked for one another. But in the next game they didn't play well and I realized that they did not know why they had won the first three matches. Some of them began to do things their own way.

'So I had to bale into them and I finally got over to them that their first priority is to get into the Thistle team and that they will not be in it unless they play for the team, not for themselves, and that means playing it my way.'

A smile creeps over Auld's face as he remembers. 'Things were going well one time with Celtic and we beat somebody 4–0. I had a right good game and in the dressing room as I kicked off my boots I was grinning and joking and feeling great. And then I saw Jock Stein's legs and looked up ready to take the congratulations modestly.

'Instead, the boss shouted at me: "What the hell did you think you were doing out there?" and as I blinked he told me of how I had tried to score myself when there were two men better placed and how I had run with the ball when I should have parted with it and how I had not run when I should have and I began to sag until I was almost under the bench.

'But it was a lesson to me and brought home the point that the player is not the judge of whether he has played well or not. The manager is the sole judge and you can play well without kicking the ball as long as you do what he has laid down for you.

Benny Rooney typifies the Thistle spirit as he gets to the ball first in a clash with Kilmarnock's Ian McCulloch.

And that's what our players at Firhill are learning.'

Anyhow Bertie set Thistle into new ways

– and it wasn't easy. After all, Auld had been deeply involved for years in the higher reaches of football and he had to simplify explanations for those who had never been within talking distances of those upper echelons.

But Bertie has certainly got his message

Jackie Campbell gives determination to the
Thistle defence.

One of the best goalkeepers in Scotland —
that's Alan Rough, of Partick Thistle.

Thistle have always been noted for their characters. Here's one, the entertaining Denis McQuade.

across as Thistle's success proved last season.

Don't think for a moment, however, that Auld is an old-style boss who feels he can only do things himself or that players must be bullied. Auld has a great respect, liking and admiration for his players. And he doesn't hesitate to say so.

'Nothing this team of mine does will surprise me,' he grins. 'It is that kind of team, capable of anything when their full potential shows through. They won the title because of their determination, enthusiasm and skill. They have been very good at their best and they can be better yet.

'They can play it hard but football as far as I am concerned is still a man's game and I expect my players to play like men, not big lassies.

'But attack whenever possible – that will always be the name of the Thistle game.'

Thistle have some of the best young players in Scotland and there is new enthusiasm for the team in Maryhill.

Now Thistle are celebrating 100 years in football for they were formed in 1876. It was a dour struggle at the start but the turning point came with the change of headquarters to Firhill. Apart from the Reids – and Miller Reid is the youngest club chairman in Scotland – the most famous name at Firhill is that of George Easton who served the Jags loyally as treasurer, secretary and manager.

But things have changed since the days of Mr Easton, who revealed that the income of the club in 1896 was £1000 and the wages bill was £323.

The permanent acquisition of Firhill by Thistle was due to a chance conversation Mr Easton had with Sir John Ure Primrose, a famous Glasgow figure. Sir John mentioned that the proprietors of the ground, the former Caledonian Railways Company, wanted to sell it – and so Thistle stepped in and bought the ground for £5500.

And now Partick Thistle, the club which has given so much pleasure to so many for a century, are set for bigger and better things under the managership of Bertie Auld.

MEET FOOTBALL'S BRAVEST MEN...
Alan Ball and other great defiers

Alan Ball, of Queen of the South, is typical of all that's great in goalkeeping. He has the heart of a lion, the eye of a hawk. He has safe hands and he has experience. And he is a fiercely loyal club-man, just as daft about the Dumfries team now as he was all those years ago when he was signed.

Alan is one of the best Queens players of all time and he is still a hero to the fans of the friendly Palmerston club.

Queen of the South chairman Willie Harkness says Alan is the best buy his club ever made – and the Dumfries boss will never forget the telephone call he put in at the coal-face at Hetton-le-Hole Colliery, County Durham – at 2 a.m.

The man at the other end of the line, 100 feet underground, was Alan Ball, then aged 19 and the goalkeeper of the local Stanley United.

Within minutes Alan was at the surface and later, over mugs of tea and corned beef sandwiches, the young Englishman signed for Queens. That was 14 years ago and now Alan Ball has played more than 600 matches for his Scottish senior club. He doesn't want to play for anyone else, this paragon of club loyalty who says:

'I've had many offers in my time at Palmerston to join other clubs but I've never been anything but happy with Queen of the South.'

Alan had his pick of more glamorous clubs than Queen of the South when chairman Harkness arrived on the scene and he could have gone to Blackpool, Aston Villa or Northampton. Later, Newcastle United and Carlisle wanted him.

'I went north, really, to become a part-time footballer so that I could complete my apprenticeship as an electrician,' he said. 'It proved the right decision and in the next eight and a half years I turned out for the Queens' first eleven without missing a single game.'

Alan Ball shows why the experts say a keeper doesn't really become good until he's past 30. Now he's 32 – and has no intention of retiring. He grins: 'Look at Ronnie Simpson and look at our own last keeper, George Farm. George played until he was 41. I reckon I've another ten years left.'

Undoubtedly keepers last longer than most players. Great keepers seem to go on for ever. Indeed, the most dubious privilege in our great game is to be the deputy to one of the truly princely keepers. They go on for ever and ever.

Alan Ball, a partner in a Dumfries car business, has seen several managers come and go at Palmerston – George Farm, Bobby Shearer, Jacky Husband, Harold Davis, Jim Easton, Willie McLean and the present chief, Mike Jackson.

And of the former Celtic player, Alan says: 'He's a man who deserves success because of the tremendous effort he puts into

High jumper Alan Ball, of Queen of the South, makes sure he holds the ball, as Rangers' Derek Johnstone stands by, hoping for a slip.

Keepers always keep an anxious eye on
that man Johnstone of Rangers. And here
Peter Latchford, of Celtic, makes a
courageous save from the keepers' enemy.

his work.' And Ball and Jackson were key figures in Queens' remarkable recovery from the brink of relegation last season to the Second Division.

Alan, of course, is only one of the Scottish keepers who do tremendous jobs for their clubs. Sometimes I feel we don't give enough praise to the goalies. After all, they are the Aunt Sallies of football, shot at from all angles on the field of play.

And it's their sad fate that these talented men are merely taken for granted, seldom praised but told they're only doing their job when they make a miraculous save.

They're the guys who stand alone. Often they're the fall guys.

But they are the bravest of the brave, the keepers. They're also the most knowledge-able, requiring to have mathematical, meteorological and psychological learning in that they must be able to bisect angles, sense what effect the wind or rain may have on the ball, and try to psyche out the possible direction of shots.

Let's look at some of our Scottish death and glory boys in action . . .

What does a keeper need most? Hands. And here you see only the hands of East Fife keeper Ernie McGarr as he foils the leaping Martin Henderson of Rangers.

Just in time. Motherwell's Stewart Rennie gets a hand out and clears as Kenny Dalglish of Celtic tries a cute back-heeler.

Whoops . . . up and over. Rangers' Peter McCloy seems to be getting a helping hand from an Ayr United player as he goes up for a ball.

Get to the ball first . . . never mind the man in the middle, whether friend or foe. And Bobby Clark, of Aberdeen, one of the finest keepers in the business, bumps both defender and attacker as he sticks to the goalie's rule and punches clear.

Hang on there, lad! And is Ayr keeper
Hugh Sproat delighted to see a shot go
over. . . .

Rangers keeper Stewart Kennedy reveals a
neat show of undershirt as he clears in a
game against Ayr United.

SIGHS FROM THE PAST CAN BRING BACK EUROPEAN GLORY

Once again Scotland made a poor showing in the major European competitions last season. And once again we all want to know why it is that football in Scotland so exciting, so dramatic, is often laughed at by the Continentals.

Is there such a gulf in technical standards? Are there two different types of soccer – that played by the British and that by the Continentals?

A résumé of the European facts in season 1975–6 kicks us painfully in the teeth. For a start we saw our Scottish League champions, Rangers, being rather off-handedly ejected from the European Cup at St Etienne.

Rangers didn't have much luck, admittedly, and their morale was sadly dented by one of the bizarre incidents in European football even before the match began.

As a vociferous 29 000 crowd swept away the fog clouds over the Guichard stadium with a tremendous volley of sound, Rangers lost goalkeeper Peter McCloy before the match kicked off. At shooting-in practice. Colin Stein blasted a ball at McCloy and the big keeper stuck out a hand – a mistake if ever there was one, for Peter injured his hand. He had to go off and on came Stewart Kennedy, making his first major appearance for Rangers since his disaster at Wembley

Rangers' Peter McCloy in action. But a bizarre accident kept the keeper out of European Cup action.

the previous season for Scotland against England.

Kennedy couldn't be blamed for the 2–0 defeat on that depressing October night of 1975. Nevertheless, the loss of a keeper who had been in top form under such peculiar circumstances and the fact that Kennedy was short of first team practice didn't help Rangers.

Anyhow, defensive blunders cost the Scots the two goals, the second of which was scored in the last minute.

But Rangers let Scotland down in the second leg at Ibrox when they were beaten 2–1 for they stumbled out of Europe with an inept display. An anticipated Fifth of November fireworks display turned out to be a damp squib and it was a night of torture for the 45 000 who turned up and loyally tried to urge on their stuttering idols.

There was no excuse for this failure and Rangers lacked the style and class to be a success in Europe – mainly because their tactics were the high cross and hopeful header . . . tactics which St Etienne countered almost disdainfully. They were pitifully old-fashioned and they left the Frenchmen laughing.

Now, St Etienne – as we saw at Hampden – turned out to be one of the greatest sides in Europe last season so it was really no disgrace for Rangers to have lost, despite the embarrasing gulf between the footballing abilities of the two sides.

And it is only fair to say that Rangers improved mightily after that European Cup defeat and who knows what the result might have been had the clubs met later in the season. The trouble is that excuses and post-mortems are for losers – and that is the sad fact we are considering : that Scotland are too often losers in Europe.

Celtic did better – but not all that much. The Parkhead club, experimenting all season and hit by influenza and injury, reached the quarter-final of the European Cup-winners Cup tournament – but failed sadly at what should have been an easy hurdle, the hardly formidable East Germans, Sachsenring Zwickau.

Zwickau turned out to be one of the worst teams seen in the tournament – but they put the accent on defence and the team who had once been the toast of Europe because of exhilarating, attacking football hadn't the ability to pierce the defence.

Celtic created a score of chances over the 180 minutes but managed only one goal at Parkhead. Uninspiring Sachsenring from a mere handful of chances scored two.

Hibernian and Dundee United went out of the UEFA Cup without creating a ripple.

There can be excuses, too, for Celtic, who had what looked like a good equalizing goal in East Germany chalked off for a reason known only to the referee.

As I said, though, excuses are never made by winners. And what we need in Scotland are winners in Europe.

What goes wrong? Perhaps it is our technique. Scottish teams still try to batter down the goals of Continental opponents, so sophisticated in defence, instead of trying to pick the lock. Scottish teams lack patience. So, of course, do Scottish crowds, who want hell-for-leather assaults which, bluntly, play right into the barrows of the other side.

Maybe our teams still look on Celtic's European Cup victory over Inter-Milan as the key. And certainly Celtic attacked with power and fury in that Lisbon final. But

Alec MacDonald was one of the best Rangers of last season.

they forget that the Lisbon Lions of Parkhead had a special magic. It wasn't only brute strength and speed – the ingredients on which so many of our clubs today pin their faith in Europe.

Certainly the Celts of Lisbon were a spectacularly exciting attacking team. But there was a potent compound in the spell over Parkhead. Perseverance was one ingredient. Jock Stein was another – Stein the master of tactics, an inspiration, a dream manager. Versatility, resilience, imagination, pace, power – all those, too, played a part in Celtic's magical roundabout.

When you really analyse it, however, and compare the glowing tapestry of Parkhead's European success with the threadbare carpet on which other Scottish sides have paraded their Continental hopes you realize that, like the top European sides, Celtic put the accent above all on artistic, thinking players. Celtic achieved European glory because they continued a rich heritage. The Parkhead formula hadn't changed.

In the great old Celtic days, the heroes were the Quinns, the McGrorys, the Delaneys, the flamboyant, extrovert, dashing scorers who made the headlines. But these stars couldn't have become the lethal finishers they were without the aid of the man of genius, the astute wing-halfs and inside forwards of craft, cunning and superb control.

Patsy Gallagher, Alex Thomson, Malcolm MacDonald, Peter Wilson – these were only some of the elegant players who had skill to set the Celtic pattern.

These were the men who made the openings.

So it was when Celtic won the European Cup in 1967. Jimmy Johnstone was a wonder of the touchline – but always making the play were Bobby Murdoch and Bertie Auld, technically perfect in the crisper soccer of the sixties but players who would have fitted brilliantly into the courtlier scene of yesteryear and who would certainly

Up and coming Alex Miller of Rangers looks forward to success in Europe soon.

have been men who would have turned the tide in Europe for Celtic had they been playing last season.

That was the Celtic magic. It was glimpsed but has never been matched since in Scotland. Celtic took the gilt of the past and welded it to the chrome of modern soccer, embellishing it with Stein's special polish.

And that's what's wrong with Scottish clubs in Europe now. They still seem to imagine power and speed and courage will terrorize the dudes of Europe. What a hope!

Continental teams are just as strong, just as fast as the Scots. They are better drilled and certainly more sophisticated. They have better players and they are more patient. They can take chances, too.

Frankly, I'd like to see more clubs give ball players a chance. In the end, only artists can make football sparkle, can bring European success. I believe we still have them, though they are becoming harder to find. But nowadays clubs put the emphasis on success. No wonder the fans are leaving. They want skill and entertainment. They receive too much depressing fare.

Many feel the reason for our non-success in Europe is merely failure to take chances. Not so, in my view. We don't have enough guile to carve those iron defences.

Perhaps Lawrie Reilly, that great Scotland and Hibernian centre-forward was right when he said last season: 'I'd hate to play with some of the present-day teams and players. They have no brains. As a centre-forward, I'd soon get fed up running into good positions and never getting the ball.

'In my day, there was no extensive coaching such as there is now, simply because it wasn't needed. We worked on general fitness and sharpness in training and, naturally, as we at Easter Road had a smallish forward line, we didn't play the high ball. It was hard and low or a chip to the near post.'

And if our Scottish teams who failed in Europe last season had concentrated more on the cut-back they might have earned honours.

But, as Lawrie Reilly says, 'There is not the same skill in the game nowadays, nor the variety of players. The players just don't work at it. There are too many distractions for youngsters. They watch television or are out on bikes or away in the family car.

'In my time we were out in the streets with a ball all the time. That's where you learned control and how to think.

'And I'd like to see players being encouraged more to express themselves freely and naturally.'

Reilly's solution to our ills in Europe is to bring back wingers. 'They are the men who make scoring easier for the other forwards. And they bring excitement to the game,' he says.

I agree with Lawrie – up to a point. But to earn success in Europe, to ensure that our teams can some day compare with Bayern Munich, Barcelona, St Etienne and the other high-rankers, we also need a new Willie Sharpe, Jimmy Williamson, Derek Grierson, Torry Gillick and George Hamilton in the teams of our contenders for the glamorous cups.

And if those of you who believe football begins and ends with all-purpose players and faceless robots want to know who these people were, I shall be glad to tell you.

These men – and scores like them – were really the men who made our soccer great. They were the lifeblood of the game. They were never known as truly great masters. But there were plenty of them. And that was why old-time football was mellow and golden because these great inside-forwards laced it with velvet passes, grace, courtliness and magical use of the open space.

Once we return to letting skilful inside-forwards and wily wingers have their heads we will have a chance of competing in Europe again on level terms with our Continental opponents.

Oh, for a new Jimmy Johnstone! He's the
type of player Celtic fans pray for nowadays.

IT'S THE SMILE THAT MEANS VICTORY

Victory always brings a smile in football – and here are some happy pictures of the season's winners.

Scotland's youth team – who had a wonderful season – run a lap of honour at Hampden.

Rangers' captain John Greig has a word with this little fan as the team run a lap of honour at Ibrox.

It's champagne for manager Bertie Auld and his merry players as they celebrate their success in winning the First Division title.

No wonder they're cheerful. This is the
Bo'ness team who won the Junior Cup
Final by beating Darvel at Hampden.